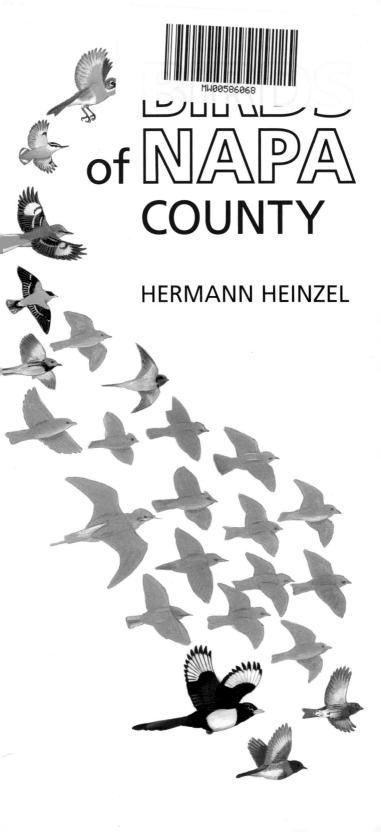

BIRDS
of NAPA
COUNTY

HERMANN HEINZEL

Published by Heyday Books
P. O. Box 9145, Berkeley, CA 94709
www.heydaybooks.com

Library of Congress Cataloging-in-Publication Data

Heinzel, Hermann.
  Birds of Napa County / Hermann Heinzel.
      p. cm.
Includes bibliographical references and index.
ISBN 1-59714-030-9 (pbk.: alk. paper)
1. Birds--California--Napa County--Identification. I. Title.
QL684.C2H45 2006
598.09794'19--dc22
                          2006011800

Pre-printing by Birgit Schroeter   Reprinted in 2021 by DAMAGRAPH
Cologne, Germany   Bilbao, Spain

Contents

Foreword

Napa County offers a broad spectrum of bird habitat. From the Napa Marsh in south county to the highest elevation of Mount St. Helena to the north (4343'), the habitat is diverse and includes the three main riparian drainage systems: the Napa River, Pope Creek and Putah Creek. On the west there is a north-south ridge with coniferous forests descending easterly to the Napa Valley floor and its vineyards. From here it continues to progress easterly over ridges with mixed oak woodlands and chaparral, falling again to the major savannah valleys of Pope and Berryessa. The Berryessa Valley is bounded on the east by the 3000' Blue Ridge escarpment.

The pine forests, oak woodlands, savannah, chaparral, lakes, salt marsh and riparian ecosystems in Napa County provide a welcome home for over 310 species of resident, migratory and accidental birds. One of the earliest records of Napa County birds indicates that a California Condor egg was collected on August 16, 1845. Putting this date in perspective would be to say that this was the period when George Yount, grizzly bears and Indians lived in the Napa Valley, before the Bear Flag r evolt.

In 2003 the Napa-Solano Audubon Society published *Breeding Birds of Napa County.* During a period of five years in the early 1990s a group of volunteer ornithologists created an atlas of the 145 confirmed nesting birds in Napa County and another 11 considered possible or probable. Swainson's Hawk was added to the confirmed list during the research for this book.

Ornithologists in Napa, as in many counties throughout the United States, annually volunteer their time to count species and populations during the Audubon Christmas Bird Count. The purpose of this census is to monitor these populations looking for population trends and therefore using the birds as a barometer to determine the health of the ecosystem. Napa County has a conscientious group of ornithologists who annually perform this duty. Many of these birders volunteered to guide the author-illustrator throughout Napa County searching for birds both rare and common. We wish to thank them for their dedicated effort and note that without their help this project would not have been completed.

Coming from France but no stranger to the United States, Hermann Heinzel was guided throughout Napa County and exposed to its birds and their habitats. Hermann is a perfectionist, a consummate artist looking for the finest detail of color, shape and feather. He wants to know every detail of the birds, their inter-relationships with other species and the habitats in which they live. I think you will agree, Hermann's effort on *Birds of Napa County* is unsurpassed and we have been privileged to have him do the work. Hermann has been the illustrator for many books including *Birds of Britain and Europe, Seabirds of the World, Galapagos Diary* and *Birds of the Bohemian Grove.*

George and Launce Gamble
Gamble Ranch
November 2006

Acknowledgements

Preparing this book has been a great pleasure. Over several weeks during Spring 2005, I spent each day in the valleys, high ridges and backcountry and along the marshes of Napa County, observing and sketching birds and their habitats. There was also ample opportunity to sample the many fine wines for which this county is justly known!

My task would have been impossible without the help and resources available to me. My thanks first of all go to George and Launce Gamble, whose sponsorship made this book possible. George, a keen birder himself, led me through the high backcountry of north county, and showed me so many of the birds I had really wanted to observe in Napa, such as my favorites, the Lewis's Woodpecker, Yellow-billed Magpie and Lawrence's Goldfinch. I was also able to study the differences between the two larger grebes and the breeding Bald Eagles. My thanks for his generous time, companionship, and hospitality. Great thanks to Mrs. Mardelle Berner, the mother of expert birder Murray Berner. I was a guest in Mardy's home almost my entire stay in the county. Mardy made me feel at home. Robin Leong, himself an expert birder, organized a truly knowledgeable group of birders who accompanied me on my daily trips. I generally left the house each day at dawn and was out until late afternoon or evening. In addition to Robin, these keen companions were Bill Grummer, Jim Hench, Mike Parmeter, Guy Kay, Phil Burton, Mike Rippey, David Bajan, Ted Wooster, Kelly and Rob Solomon, Jane Mead and Richard Reissman. All were generous with their time. Collectively it would be difficult to find another group with such deep knowledge of birding in the county. My personal thanks go to each. I must acknowledge an excellent book that was extremely useful to my preparation: *Breeding Birds of Napa County*, a publication of the Napa-Solano Audubon Society. Maureen Flannery at the California Academy of Sciences was helpful while I researched the song sparrow subspecies.

Roderick Hall, who implanted in me a love of California, was the catalyst for this book. His constant support and generous time were essential contributions to this entire project. Warmest thanks for this volunteer. This is the third book we have worked on together. Rod put me in contact with the Gambles and assembled the widely dispersed team that has made this book a reality: Malcolm Margolin and Rebecca LeGates at Heyday Books in Berkeley, California, the publishers; Angel Sanchez of Estudios Gráficos Zure in Bilbao, Spain, the printers; and Birgit Schroeter in Cologne, Germany, who converted my layout, text and paintings into the digital format printers work with today. Thanks to Murray Berner, who contributed his knowledge of Napa County and its birds. Maggie Sweetnam in London typed my manuscript and corrected my fractured English with patience. Warm thanks to all, and *merci a Colette Demblans et Isabelle Morvan de la Mairie de Lombez pour leur precieuse aide technique*. A truly international effort.

Hermann Heinzel
Gers, Southwest France
November 2006

Introduction This book provides a basic introduction to the avifauna of Napa County. Napa is fortunate in having a rich and varied population of birds. About 310 species have been recorded and more than 150 species are regular breeders in the county. Others are guests, mostly from the north, that winter here. Some are rare occasional vagrants from all over North America, or perhaps lost wanderers from Asia. All are included in this book. One bird subspecies is found only in Napa and in the neighboring counties on San Pablo Bay (p. 113). For many birds, Napa is an important area in which to breed; for even more birds it is a place to overwinter.

avifauna:
the entire birdlife of an area

population:
all birds living in one area or a specified place

species:
a distinct kind of plant or animal

breeders:
birds that breed in the county

habitat:
the natural home environment of an animal or bird

I particularly enjoy helping people develop an interest in birdlife, and therefore this book is based on illustrations. I like, to show as much as possible of each bird species, the different plumages and some of their habits, but space was limited. This book is a lightweight guide to take into the field. An illustration tells so much more than a long, dry description. Identifying a bird is often straightforward, but some species can be difficult even for the expert. Start by identifying birds around your home. When you know them, you can compare them with a new bird. It's not only the plumage that identifies the bird. Habitat, song, behavior, and even the time of year assist identification. One learns with patience.

Where Birds Live Although very mobile, most birds have adapted to living in certain surroundings, or habitats. Some species are more particular about their location, but all are influenced by such factors as the availability of the food they require, nesting sites, cover and protection, or even simply song posts. Adaptation to habitat developed slowly during evolution, starting with food supply and nesting sites. Other adaptations came later. The many different types of habitat in Napa County include not only chaparral, grassland, oak woodlands, marshes, lakes and rivers, but also vineyards and urban areas (see p. 10-11). One soon gets to know the birds likely to be seen given the habitat.

Some bird names make it easy to recognize their habitats. House Finches and the introduced House Sparrow will most likely be found around houses, in towns or on farms, as long as there is a food supply. The Meadowlark is best found on dry meadows and similar grassland; on Rock Wrens are near or on rocks. Everyone knows ducks need water to swim. A Mallard can be found nesting even in a small ditch if there is cover for the nest. Scaup need deep open water to dive for food and Mergansers need clear running streams for fishing. Birds of prey cover vast areas, but Osprey will never be seen far from open water except when flying from one area to another. Accipiter Hawks (p. 37) are always in dense woodland or its edges, but on migration will fly across open mountain ridges. Harriers are grassland specialists. Red-shouldered Hawks, while more general in habitat, prefer open woodland with tall trees in which to nest and snags on which to perch while hunting. Kestrels are found primarily in ranch country. The Spotted Owl will only live in wooded, shady canyons with old-growth conifers and oak, but the Great Horned Owl will hunt at night even within the city of Napa. Change and destruction of habitat can influence the resident bird community, even driving some to extinction.

Many birds are named after their habitat or color, such as this bluebird. Living only in the West, it is called the Western Bluebird.

Getting to Know the Birds All worthwhile birding is based on correct identification, and knowing what to expect is half the game. The drawings in this book show many features not described for lack of space. The thick bill of a seed-eating sparrow, for example, is quite different from an insect-eating warbler's thin bill. In addition to obvious differences in size, structure and coloring, one can learn to identify them by both **habits** and **habitat**. For a beginner, all little brown birds such as sparrows, wrens and female warblers look similar. Watching for patterns, spots, stripes, bars, etc., will reveal the identity. With waders, ducks and soaring hawks, it is particularly useful to know the different patterns displayed during flight.

The different wing and tail patterns and colors identify the hawk in flight.

Song Early each year the flocks of sparrows, finches and others that have fed together in the fields or at bird feeders show signs of breaking up. Males will chase each other and sing snatches of their song. Birds return from their winter quarters in the south and soon will be calling and singing from every bush and tree. Meadowlarks and red-wings that nest in open country often sing in flight. Woodpeckers 'drum' by hammering rapidly against a dry branch or even telephone pole. It is not easy to describe the songs. Does a Killdeer call 'deeye' or 'tyeee,' 'kil-deeah' or is it more like 'kill-dee' or really a shrill 'kill-deer'? All the same call, described by different listeners. Tapes and CDs of bird songs are readily available.

A rooster's song is heard and described differently. English: 'Cock-a-doodle-doo' German: 'Kikeriki' French: 'Cocorico'

Courtship With smaller birds, the first stage is usually the male's song, often combined with a special flight, such as the red-wings puffing up their brilliant red epaulettes (p. 100). The famous ballet-like dance of the Western and Clark's Grebes is spectacular and easy to observe as they display on open water (p. 19). Hawks soar high in the air over their territory, calling loudly, often performing acrobatic dives at high speed. Ducks, before departing for their more northern breeding grounds, will often court together in flocks: one male starts posturing, others follow to show their bright colors and patterns, all to impress the females who finally join in. While the displays may seem to consist of a number of apparently trivial items, all form part of a complex inherited ritual designed to attract females and make sure that both male and female are ready to breed at the same time.

The strutting posture of a displaying gobbler.

Territory The territory needed by each pair in order to breed differs greatly among the various species. A couple of robins can raise their brood in a garden, while a pair of Golden Eagles needs a vast territory of many square miles, depending on the availability of food. Both species will defend their territory fiercely against any food competitor. Others, such as terns, herons or Tricolored Blackbirds live and breed in colonies, and are content with privacy only around their nest, but feed separately outside the communal breeding territory. Spacing out breeding pairs has the effect of dividing the available habitats and food more evenly, according to the needs of each species, allowing each pair to rear their young. Many species return each year to the same territory. The Golden Eagle defends its territory throughout the year.

territory: small or large area defended by the male or pairs

Nest Most birds build a new nest each season and never use the previous year's nest. Herons and hawks repair and redecorate their old nests, while owls and falcons build no nest at all, laying their eggs in a cavity or hollow scrape on a cliff. The role played by the male and female in choosing a nesting site and building the nest varies greatly from species to species.

The Killdeer's very simple nest, a shallow scrape.

Bird eggs vary greatly in size, shape and color.

clutch size:
the number of eggs laid in one brood

precocial:
active immediately, downy chicks follow their parents after hatching

parasitic:
birds that lay their eggs in the nests of other species

incubating:
a parent sitting on eggs to supply the heat needed for development of the embryo

Related birds can often live in the same habitat by using different parts of it.

migration:
when birds move, often in large numbers, from one region to another to breed or overwinter

Eggs & breeding Once the nest is ready, the female starts to lay until the clutch is complete. Clutch size varies from 1-3 eggs for birds of prey, such as the Red-tailed Hawk or Bald Eagle, to up to 15 or even 28 for California Quail. Clutch size is based on such factors as the number of young the parents can feed and the number that may perish before becoming adults. Species that produce precocial young tend to lay larger clutches than birds such as warblers or sparrows that feed their youngsters in the nest and, like most songbirds, only lay 3 to 5 eggs. Titmice lay 5-8 and a parasitic Cowbird lays up to 30 in one season. Egg size and markings also differ widely: from .5x.35 in. for Anna's Hummingbird up to 3x2.3 in. for the egg of the Golden Eagle. Markings are not always for concealment, though some, such as Avocet or Killdeer eggs, are marvellously camouflaged. Most hole-nesting birds, such as woodpeckers and owls, and tree nesting doves lay white eggs. Songbirds usually incubate their eggs 12-14 days, hummingbirds 16 days, most ducks 26-29 and eagles up to 46 days. Generally the female alone incubates, but with some species both parents take their turn. Spotted Sandpiper females lay several clutches and males alone care for them. All ducks when hatched are already downy, active, mobile and can feed themselves. Songbird chicks and many others are helpless, and may remain in the nest, fed by their parents until they fledge and fly away.

Food Most birds are restricted to some extent by the food they eat. A robin will take insects, worms and berries. Warblers eat only insects; sparrows eat seeds but rear their brood with insects. Ravens and crows will eat almost anything, cormorants mostly fish, and owls eat rodents. Nearly all specialize in some way. A titmouse will eat about a quarter of its own weight (0.6 oz.) per day while a large hawk may average 4%. Physical structure has much to do with diet and how it is obtained: chickadees can forage along the thinnest twigs while the heavier Oak Titmouse feeds around the larger branches or trunk. Some, like grebes or scaups, are specialist divers and take their food underwater. The beaks of all birds are adapted to their food and methods of feeding, even in species like the Curlew, where the female has a longer bill than the male, or the Avocet, where the bend of bill is different in the sexes. Woodpeckers have chisel-like bills to drill into wood. Osprey have specially designed feet to hold their slimy prey while transporting it to a safe place to eat or to the nest to feed the youngsters. Songbird young are fed mainly on insects carried in the bill, Corvids (p. 78-79) that are also songbirds bring food to the young pouched in the throat, and regurgitate it. Finch nestlings are usually fed on regurgitated seeds from their parent's crop.

Migration is a well-known phenomenon, but there is still much to learn about why and how birds orient themselves on their way. It is not the cold that causes birds to migrate, but the shortage of food and the length of daylight. Most Napa birds can be classified as summer or winter visitors, passage migrants or residents, but some species fall into several of these categories. Mallard can be seen year-round, but during fall many more arrive from the north and east, remain all winter and depart again in spring. Many waders are often just migrants, passing through in spring and fall, but some remain to winter in the county, large flocks in some years. The spring migration, when most birds are pressing north towards their breeding grounds, is a shorter and better defined movement than the gradual drift south in fall. By end of July the first wanderers have already arrived in the marshes although birds that breed in the far north may not reach Napa until November. During winter there is a good deal of local movement in response to weather conditions, and flocking becomes a feature of bird life.

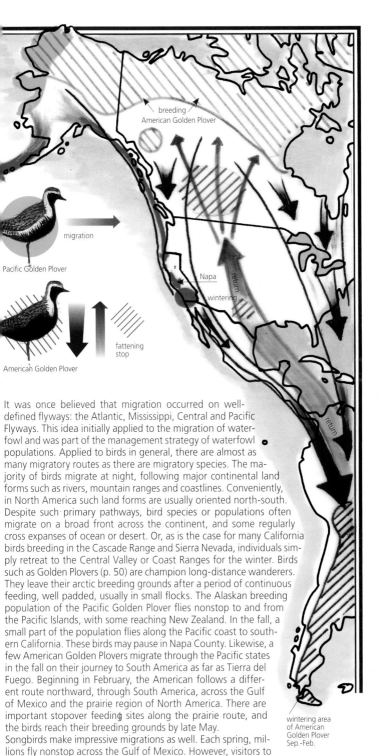

breeding
American Golden Plover

migration

Pacific Golden Plover

Napa

return

wintering

fattening
stop

American Golden Plover

return

It was once believed that migration occurred on well-defined flyways: the Atlantic, Mississippi, Central and Pacific Flyways. This idea initially applied to the migration of waterfowl and was part of the management strategy of waterfowl populations. Applied to birds in general, there are almost as many migratory routes as there are migratory species. The majority of birds migrate at night, following major continental land forms such as rivers, mountain ranges and coastlines. Conveniently, in North America such land forms are usually oriented north-south. Despite such primary pathways, bird species or populations often migrate on a broad front across the continent, and some regularly cross expanses of ocean or desert. Or, as is the case for many California birds breeding in the Cascade Range and Sierra Nevada, individuals simply retreat to the Central Valley or Coast Ranges for the winter. Birds such as Golden Plovers (p. 50) are champion long-distance wanderers. They leave their arctic breeding grounds after a period of continuous feeding, well padded, usually in small flocks. The Alaskan breeding population of the Pacific Golden Plover flies nonstop to and from the Pacific Islands, with some reaching New Zealand. In the fall, a small part of the population flies along the Pacific coast to southern California. These birds may pause in Napa County. Likewise, a few American Golden Plovers migrate through the Pacific states in the fall on their journey to South America as far as Tierra del Fuego. Beginning in February, the American follows a different route northward, through South America, across the Gulf of Mexico and the prairie region of North America. There are important stopover feeding sites along the prairie route, and the birds reach their breeding grounds by late May.

Songbirds make impressive migrations as well. Each spring, millions fly nonstop across the Gulf of Mexico. However, visitors to Napa County need not be quite as adventurous; the majority move south of the border to Mexico and Central America.

wintering area
of American
Golden Plover
Sep.-Feb.

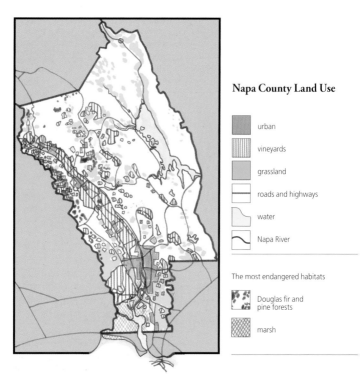

Napa County Land Use

- urban
- vineyards
- grassland
- roads and highways
- water
- Napa River

The most endangered habitats

- Douglas fir and pine forests
- marsh

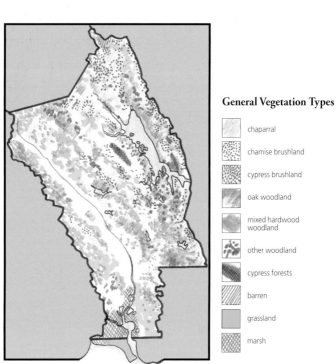

General Vegetation Types

- chaparral
- chamise brushland
- cypress brushland
- oak woodland
- mixed hardwood woodland
- other woodland
- cypress forests
- barren
- grassland
- marsh

Napa County, approximately 780 square miles in area, is one of the smaller counties in California. Lying at the margins of three biological regions, it has a very diverse and rich breeding avifauna and is an important place for wintering birds. The south, with its limited fresh and saltwater marshes near San Pablo Bay, is influenced by the wide San Francisco Bay delta with its extensive estuaries. The east lies on the edge of the open Sacramento Valley, separated by the dry Rocky and Blue ridges. The western border ranges from sea level at the Napa Slough over the ridges of the Arrowhead and Mayacamas Mountains to 4,343 ft. at Mount St. Helena. The most populated area is Napa Valley along the Napa River, with the city of Napa and the towns of Yountville, St. Helena and Calistoga the main centers. There are smaller towns such as Angwin, Oakville and Rutherford; also notable is the southern city of American Canyon, and the resort communities at Lake Berryessa. In 2000, Napa County had a population of 125,000 inhabitants. This is greatly augmented by over 2 million annual visitors.

From European settlement and continuing to the present day, the Napa County landscape has changed dramatically. Following the break-up of the Spanish land grants, settlers began the conversion of the valleys to fruit, nut, grain and livestock production. Cattle and sheep grazed the wooded hillsides from Knoxville to Carneros. Logging in the county removed primarily redwood and Douglas fir.

Following World War II, large lakes like Hennessey and Berryessa were created by dams, while the marshes were dried and turned into grassland or taken over by the salt industry. Now all is changing again. The valley has become primarily vineyards that are creeping slowly up the hillsides into forest and savannah. Ranching is declining and some grassland in the northeast is slowly reverting to woodland. Marshes have been restored. The higher, wet areas on the western boundaries are still dominated by mostly second-growth Douglas fir and coastal redwoods integrating to mixed coniferous and mixed hardwood forests. In the drier parts, chaparral and broadleaf woodland with oak savannah are still present with grassland and, in the cooler parts, vineyards. Cypress brushland and forests have always been rare and need special soil. With the landscape changes, the avifauna have also changed. The large California Condor was extirpated, followed almost unnoticed by the Yellow-billed Cuckoo. The Yellow-breasted Chat is now very rare. Other birds, like the California Quail, blackbirds, and the House Finch and Lesser Goldfinch have expanded and are now abundant. The Red-tailed Hawk has taken advantage of the changes and is now more widespread than ever. Canada Geese, once limited winter visitors, now breed throughout the county. The European House Sparrow and Starling were introduced in the northeastern U.S., have colonized the country and are now regarded as pests. After initial failure, the Turkey is now successful wherever woodland provides food and cover. The cowbird, possibly once absent, is now a summer resident and, as elsewhere in the U.S., has contributed to the decline of several local songbirds. Hummingbirds have spread with the planting of exotic flowering shrubs and trees. Raptors, now recovering from pesticide poisoning and hunting, are again playing an important role in nature.

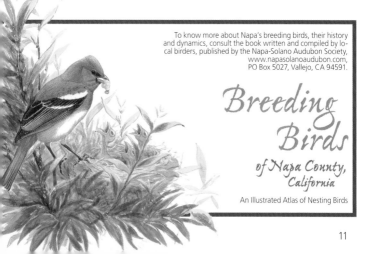

To know more about Napa's breeding birds, their history and dynamics, consult the book written and compiled by local birders, published by the Napa-Solano Audubon Society, www.napasolanoaudubon.com, PO Box 5027, Vallejo, CA 94591.

Breeding
Birds
of Napa County,
California

An Illustrated Atlas of Nesting Birds

Identifying birds is observation of details, size, shape, colors and including patterns, as with these two wrens: eyebrows, belly color, wing pattern, tail length.

A Droll-Yankee feeder with thistle seed, the favorite small-black seeds for Goldfinches and Siskins.

Watching Birds Birding can be an exciting pastime. A great deal may be learned about behavior, seasonal plumage and migration simply by watching birds in a garden or park. Making regular visits to a favorite birding location will develop a familiarity with a relatively small number of species–a starting background before tackling the hundreds found in Napa County and beyond. Keeping written notes of observations is useful. Learning the birds requires patience. Don't expect to identify every bird seen the first time. Study the field guide. Learn from an experienced friend or join the local Audubon chapter and attend their field trips. There one can learn more about good birding locations, techniques and equipment. The primary birding technique is getting into the field early when the birds are most active. Of course, a good pair of binoculars is essential. A rule of thumb is to purchase the very best that one can afford. Good binoculars, well cared for, will last a long time. Birders favor 8 to 10 magnification. For serios birding, a spotting scope and tripod is a must. I use a Swarovski El 8x32 for the smaller birds in bushes and their telescope ATS 80 on a tripod with a variable eyepiece 20-60x when observing over a long distance or while painting birds. Birders even dress a little differently, avoiding noisy raincoats and favoring muted colors and waterproof footwear.

Feeding-station One can attract birds by feeding them and by encouraging them to nest in nest boxes. After the late summer molt, many birds can be induced to come quite close to the windows of houses by a suitably sited bird-table kept supplied with the right food. The first birds to arrive at a new feeding station will most likely be House Finches and Brewer's Blackbirds. The very common and bossy House Sparrows are often more cautious, but once they see birds feeding they will take over. Several species of sparrows can be expected and one can study their differences. Titmice, robins, jays, juncos, towhees, goldfinches, quail and Mourning Doves are all regular guests at feeding stations and need different food. Black or striped sunflower is the favorite seed of many species such as House Finches, nuthatches, titmice and many others. Pine Siskin and Lesser and American Goldfinches like thistle seed. Sparrows prefer canary seed, millet and oat groats. I prefer to give the seed separately, and not in a ready-made mixture which contains many seeds birds don't like. Seed not eaten lies on the ground with birds hopping over it. This can cause disease to spread. Avoid seed such as canola, flax and rolled oats as they easily get soaked with water and not many birds like them when alternatives are available. Sweet apples and dry raisins are appreciated by many birds such as jays, orioles, tanagers, robins, etc. Beef suet is a suitable food in winter for all insect-eating birds. Household scraps should be avoided. There are some good books on this subject that detail many ways to present food to the birds living in the area, such as hopper-type feeders, Droll-Yankee feeders or just feeding on the ground. Everything should be clean, not fancy. When birds come to the feeder, notes should be kept on species and what they eat.

Feeding Hummingbirds Hummingbirds are very popular with everyone. The best way to attract them is still to plant the right flowers, such as larkspur, gladiolus, trumpet creeper, petunias and morning glory, to name a few. Even with an artificial feeder, one should plant flowers. Most feeders on the market are good. The important thing is the right syrup formula. A good, widely used formula is one part sugar and four parts water. An important feature of a hummingbird feeder is the ease of cleaning.

'Hummers' at natural flowers and vial.

Nest Boxes Everyone with a garden can help cavity-nesting birds by hanging nest boxes. The best model for smaller birds is the bluebird box type, also accepted by the Violet-green and Tree Swallows, White-breasted Nuthatch, Oak Titmouse, House Wren and the aggressive House Sparrow. If the entrance hole is too large, unwelcome starlings will occupy them. Emily Heaton at the University of California, Berkeley, has made an extensive study of nest boxes in vineyards that is worth reading (eheaton@nature.berkeley.edu). Large boxes for Barn Owl and Wood Duck seen around vineyards and the Napa River were placed by professionals and have been very successful in Napa County. Kestrel have benefited from the nest box program as well. The box should be of the proper depth with an entrance hole of the appropriate size.

All nest boxes should be cleaned after the breeding season, as old nesting material is often full of parasites. As part of the normal cycle, birds need to build fresh new nests in the next breeding season.

Bird Protection Feeders and nest boxes in gardens are a help for some species. Real help begins with habitat protection, as many natural habitats have almost disappeared, and all that still exists should be rigorously protected. There is a shortage of resources for such activities and land for nature reserves, so the best use should be made of what still remains. It is also important to understand the key needs of birds.

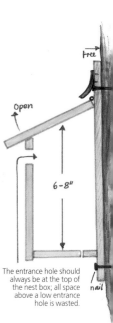

The entrance hole should always be at the top of the nest box; all space above a low entrance hole is wasted.

Protection of rare species takes a great deal of the conservationist's time. Often it is difficult to define what is a rare species. It can be argued that there are no rare birds in Napa. While only a few pairs of the Yellow-breasted Chat breed in the county, many more breed in other regions from California to the East Coast. However, the Spotted Owl is rare everywhere. It is very important to preserve the few remaining pairs of both species in the county by improving or at least protecting their habitat. Large and small areas have been put aside as parks or wildlife refuges, and much work has been done to repair degradation in the marshes, but even more can be done.

Illustrating Birds

Many have asked how I go about painting birds. Do I use a camera, and why not use photographs for this book? Well, I am not very good with anything technical such as cameras, and taking good quality photos to illustrate the sexes and all the plumages for a portable field book would make it impractically long and heavy. Fieldwork is my first step when preparing a book; observation, observation, patience, sketching, and taking notes on all the birds. Observing birds is both work and a great pleasure for me.

A good pair of binoculars is very important to spot the bird and for first observations. When sketching, I use my telescope, with an angled rather than a straight eyepiece. This allows me to look into the scope and draw at the same time. Normally I use a 20-60xS zoom eyepiece. For distant observations of, for instance, waders, I use a 45xSW eyepiece which is less tiring for the eyes. It is very important that the scope is fixed on a stable tripod. Sketches are drawn very quickly, using pencils and finely pointed waterproof felt pens and, time permitting, my small watercolor box to capture the colors of the live bird. Field notes around the sketches are most important. These sketches are not artwork but references for further work. Sometimes only part of a bird is drawn. I particularly like to capture behavior, such as a courting turkey or, as shown, a calling quail.

I generally use museum skins for color details during final work. The art for this book was done in watercolor, gouache and sometimes acrylic for brightly colored birds. The brushes used are as important as the paint and must be of the best quality. Acrylic is a difficult medium that wears out a sable brush very quickly, and synthetic brushes are just not good to work with. I use the whitest paper with a surface that is not too smooth but also without texture; it has to take paint quickly.

Some extracts from different pages of my Napa County sketchbook

Napa County Place Names

This is a list of some important, easily located sites in the county where birds can be found. USGS topographical maps are available (see below).

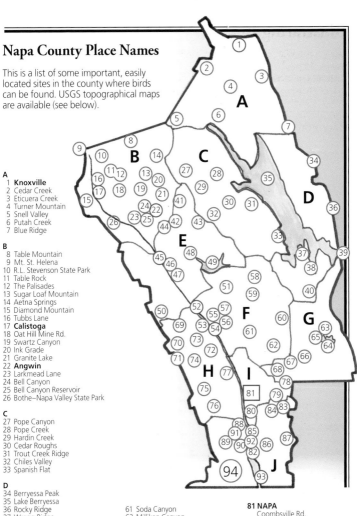

A
1 **Knoxville**
2 Cedar Creek
3 Eticuera Creek
4 Turner Mountain
5 Snell Valley
6 Putah Creek
7 Blue Ridge

B
8 Table Mountain
9 Mt. St. Helena
10 R.L. Stevenson State Park
11 Table Rock
12 The Palisades
13 Sugar Loaf Mountain
14 Aetna Springs
15 Diamond Mountain
16 Tubbs Lane
17 **Calistoga**
18 Oat Hill Mine Rd.
19 Swartz Canyon
20 Ink Grade
21 Granite Lake
22 **Angwin**
23 Larkmead Lane
24 Bell Canyon
25 Bell Canyon Reservoir
26 Bothe–Napa Valley State Park

C
27 Pope Canyon
28 Pope Creek
29 Hardin Creek
30 Cedar Roughs
31 Trout Creek Ridge
32 Chiles Valley
33 Spanish Flat

D
34 Berryessa Peak
35 Lake Berryessa
36 Rocky Ridge
37 Wragg Ridge
38 Wragg Valley
39 Monticello Dam
40 Capell Valley

E
41 Howell Mountain
42 Linda Falls
43 Las Posadas State Forest
44 Deer Park Rd.
45 **St. Helena**
46 Zinfandel Lane
47 Rutherford Quarry
48 Conn Valley
49 Lake Hennessey
50 Mt. St. John

F
51 Rector Canyon
52 **Oakville**
53 Yountville Hills
54 **Yountville**
55 Crossroad Bridge
56 Napa River
   Ecological Reserve
57 Stags Leap
58 Atlas Peak
59 Foss Valley
60 Circle Oaks

61 Soda Canyon
62 Milliken Canyon

G
63 Vaca Mountains
64 Lake Curry
65 Gordon Valley
66 Wooden Valley
67 Mt. George
68 Sarco Creek

H
69 Oakville Grade
70 Mt. Veeder
71 Hogback Mountain
72 Pickle Canyon
73 Dry Creek
74 Redwood Canyon
75 Partrick Rd.
76 Carneros Valley
77 Alston Park

I
78 Wild Horse Valley
79 Murphy Creek
80 Kennedy Park

81 NAPA
   Coombsville Rd.
   Fuller Park
   Imola Av.
   Napa Valley College
   State Hospital
   Tulocay Cemetery

J
82 Napa River
83 Spencer Creek
84 Lake Marie
85 Suscol Creek
86 North Kelly Rd.
87 Jamieson Canyon
88 Stanly Lane
89 Buchli Station
90 Cuttings Wharf
91 Napa Water
   Treatment Plant
92 Napa Airport
93 **American Canyon**
94 **Marshes**
   Coon Island
   Edgerley Island
   Fagan Slough
   Fly Bay
   Island 2
   Little Island
   Milton Rd.
   Russ Island

I used U.S. Geological Survey maps. For the south, **Napa;** for the north, **Healdsburg,** both 1:100,000. For driving: **Santa Rosa,** 1:250,000, which has good detail.

Key to Codes, Maps and Abbreviations

To make this book easily accessible, specialist jargon has been kept to a minimum. The few technical terms and abbreviations used are explained below. The topography of a bird (the different terms relating to their feather tracts) is explained on the opposite page.

Abbreviations around the pictures,
also used in the text to save space:

♂ male   ♂♂ males
♀ female   ♀♀ females

ad   adult: bird in definitive full plumage after molt

juv   juvenile: a fledged young, still wearing first plumage, not yet molted

imm   immature: wearing any non-adult plumage; In principle, still a young bird

1ˢᵗ winter etc. denotes age; also called life year system. Most birds have their full ad. plumage after one year, others, like some large gulls, only after the 3ʳᵈ winter

br   breeding: an ad.. in freshly molted-breeding plumage

nbr   nonbreeding: plumage after the autumn molt, also called winter plumage

Feb-Sep   months in which this plumage is shown

May-Aug   molting birds can show intermediate plumage

●   the start of a new family, followed by the English and scientific names

●   a division to mark a particular group within a family, e.g., in waders, the small sandpipers

sp   species; number denotes species on Napa list

Pied-billed Grebe
The standard name used in the American Ornithologists' Union (AOU) check-list of North American birds.

Podilymbus podiceps
the scientific name (always shown in italics)

---

cW, uS   abundance and status codes for the species in Napa County

Key to codes:
c   common or abundant; seen most days

f   fairly common; seen in more than 50% of days

u   uncommon; seen less than 50% of days

r   rare; seldom observed

x   extremely rare; only a few records in the county

---

e   extirpated; once bred, e.g., the California Condor now disappeared

---

i   irregular; sporadic occurrence

l   limited; found in a very limited area within the county

P   permanent resident and confirmed breeder

S   summer resident and confirmed breeder

nbr   nonbreeding; a resident (P or S bird) but not a confirmed breeder

T   transient, occurring regularly in an established range during migration

V   vagrant occurring irregularly and outside normal migration routes

W   winter resident or visitor in Jan.-Feb.

Wbr   breeds in winter, such as Anna's Hummingbird

a   autumn status, a transient or vagrant

s   spring status for a transient or vagrant when different from the status in autumn

t   assumed breeder; undoubtedly breeds but positive evidence of breeding is lacking

---

The small map, only for breeding birds, gives a good impression of breeding distribution in the county. A full red spot is for a probable or confirmed breeding site, an open circle for a possible breeding site.

The bar on the right, in some cases the left of the map, indicates by width of the stroke the species, occurrence during the year, and an idea of their abundance.

L   length (size) of the species, in inches, from bill tip to the end of the tail

ws   wingspan, the width of outstretched wings; mostly used for raptors, to indicate the differences in size when in flight

Habitat: Only used for breeding birds to name their preferred home and where they build their nest

The short text thereafter, or for nonbreeding birds following their size, points out some interesting features of the species in Napa County, such as where they originate, where they go and where they spend the winter. I avoid repeating details of plumage shown in the pictures.

Bird Topography

The basic rules for identifying a bird are few and simple. It is helpful to memorize the names of the various parts of a bird. A good way to learn the terminology and understand a bird's **topography** is to draw a bird with the help of the pictures below and to add the correct names.

Describing a bird flying away with a white bottom is a common mistake for beginners. Be sure this means it had a white **rump.** When hearing a description of a gray bird with a long bill and pale **secondaries,** seen in the marshes, one can be sure it was a **dowitcher.**

Most ducks look very similar in flight but have distinctive wing marks which are often bright and different on upper and under wings. Dabbling ducks like **Teals** and **Wigeons** have brilliant shiny 'mirrors' on their secondaries. Diving ducks, for example **Goldeneyes** or **Bluebills** or **Scaup,** have black, white and grayish patterns.

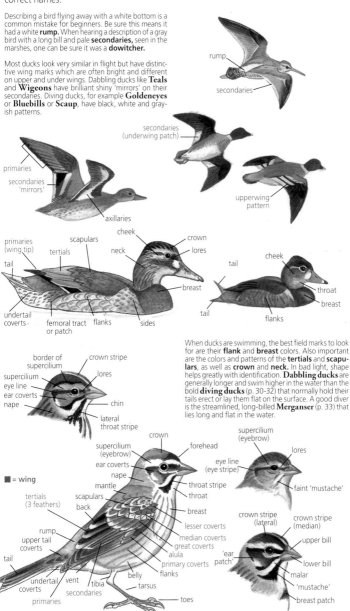

When ducks are swimming, the best field marks to look for are their **flank** and **breast** colors. Also important are the colors and patterns of the **tertials** and **scapulars,** as well as **crown** and **neck.** In bad light, shape helps greatly with identification. **Dabbling ducks** are generally longer and swim higher in the water than the bold **diving ducks** (p. 30-32) that normally hold their tails erect or lay them flat on the surface. A good diver is the streamlined, long-billed **Merganser** (p. 33) that lies long and flat in the water.

■ = wing

Topography of a Bird The same technical terms are used for large and small birds. A beginner may find it hard to remember all these technical terms, but using correct terminology augments the accuracy of notes. A clear description, with notes on behavior and habitat, will help an expert solve problems of identification.

At first glance all **Sparrows** (p. 94-97) are little brown birds. As with many **Warblers** (p. 91-93) head pattern is a very important identification point. Notice that juveniles, and nonbreeding plumages are often dull, as seen above on the head of the **Chipping Sparrow,** compared with the same bird on p. 94.

The rather large floating nest is built of rotting, soggy plant material and anchored on growing vegetation.

br Feb-Sep

juv

nbr Sep-Mar
During the breeding period the stout thick bill is white with a black ring; otherwise it is pale and dull.

• **Grebes** *Podicipedidae*, 6 sp. Highly specialized aquatic birds. Excellent divers but ungainly on land. Wings short and narrow. Rarely seen in flight, which is weak and hurried after a long take-off. Food: small fish and other aquatic life.

Pied-billed Grebe — cW, uS
Podilymbus podiceps

L 13" **Habitat:** Small ponds, reservoirs, sloughs and freshwater lakes with dense aquatic vegetation. Also on estuary waters in the marshes. Not known to breed on Lake Berryessa.

A small, stocky, drab brown grebe. Shy and retiring, it escapes by diving and hides behind aquatic vegetation. Mostly solitary or in pairs. During the breeding season it is bold and aggressive with all swimming birds. Sometimes seen in small groups out of breeding season. Often heard before being seen. The voice is a peculiar gobbling, like 'kuh-kuh-cow-cow-cow cowp Ku-Kwop.'

Horned Grebe — rW
Podiceps auritus

L 14" A common winter visitor along the California Pacific coast but rarely observed in Napa County as they prefer deep open seawater. In spring it's a good idea to look for them on Lake Berryessa. Single birds visit Napa waters, arriving hidden in the large flocks of wintering Eared Grebes. Slightly larger, about the size of a teal, with a longer thicker neck and straight dark bill with a pale tip. The flat dark cap, with peak at the rear, is typical.

br Apr-Aug

nbr Sep-Mar
Compared to the duller, dark-cheeked Eared Grebes, they stand out, looking very clean with their pure white cheeks and contrasting black cap.

1st w Sep-Apr

nbr Sep-Mar

br. Feb.-Aug:
When in breeding plumage, readily identifiable with pale gray cheeks (darker in older birds) and rufous neck.

Red-necked Grebe — ixW
Podiceps grisegena

L 18" A coastal bird recorded once in Napa County. Usually stays away from the shore and some might go unrecognized in a flock of other Grebes. They are much larger and longer bodied than the Horned but smaller than the thin-necked Western or Clark's Grebes, with a strong, dull yellowish bill. Usually silent like all Grebes in winter, but very vocal when breeding further north.

nbr Oct-Mar

br Apr-Sep
Some remain all year and can be observed in this beautiful breeding plumage with black neck and wispy golden-yellow ear plumes.

Eared Grebe — cW, lrS
Podiceps nigricollis

L 13" Each winter at least 1,000 Eared Grebes mingle with diving and dabbling ducks at the larger ponds of southern Napa County. Smaller and dumpy, but more delicate than the other two visiting grebes and the stocky Pied-billed. It has a typically thin, slightly upturned bill, a thinner neck and peaked crown. Dark cheeks and usually a dusky neck.

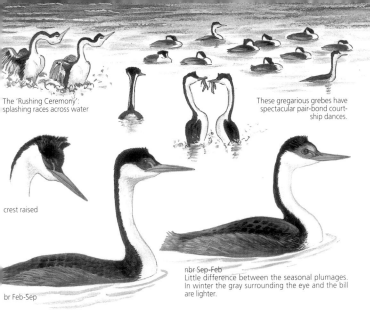

The 'Rushing Ceremony': splashing races across water

These gregarious grebes have spectacular pair-bond courtship dances.

crest raised

nbr Sep-Feb
Little difference between the seasonal plumages. In winter the gray surrounding the eye and the bill are lighter.

br Feb-Sep

Large, strikingly black and white grebe with graceful long neck. Pointed, slightly upturned, thin spear-like bill. Highly social. Usually seen on well-spaced rafts in open water, never closely packed like ducks. Concentrate in large numbers on good feeding grounds with abundant small fish. Seems they depend more on fish than other grebes, often diving for over 30 seconds. Since the right habitat is limited, breeding colonies in Napa are small, with only 25 nests in the largest colony. When the water level is low, they don't reproduce.

Western Grebe
Aechmophorus occidentalis

cw, IuS

L 25" **Habitat:** They prefer large freshwater lakes such as Berryessa and Hennessey, where a few pairs are resident and hundreds spend the winter. Breeding in colonies, they need long shorelines with high, dense aquatic vegetation to hide their floating nests. Any disturbance should be avoided since they readily abandon their nests. A few may breed on Lake Curry.

◁ Intermediate birds, believed to be crosses between the Western and Clark's Grebe, are occasionally seen. I observed one on Lake Berryessa and from its shape and habit, it looked more like an abberant Clark's than a hybrid.

Only the area surrounding the eyes was darker; body color was more like a Clark's, with a strong yellowish bill.

nbr Sep-Feb
As with the Western, there is little change between breeding and nonbreeding plumage. When breeding, eyebrow becomes more gray but not below the eyes.

br Feb-Sep

Recently it was realized that the Clark's and Western Grebe were two different species. Previously the Clark's was thought to be a color variant of the Western. Habits, courtship dances, breeding, etc. are similar but not identical. Voices are also similar but the Clark's call is a higher-pitched croak, a loud single 'Krrik,' while the Western's call is a loud, two-note 'krree-Kreeet,' similar to a Kildeer.

Clark's Grebe
Aechmophorus clarkii

IP

L 25" **Habitat:** Same as the Western but appear to prefer deeper water, smaller fish and aquatic insects. Napa birds are usually resident but, like the Western with which they form mixed colonies, breeding is irregular, depending on the water level and vegetation. Less common than the Western Grebe.

19

● **Loons** *Gaviidae* 3 sp. Large, bulky cigar-shaped swimmers. Superficially they resemble the larger grebes but have longer bodies, shorter thick necks and dagger-like bills.

nbr Nov-Mar

br Feb-Oct

juv Aug.
Resembling the ad. nbr. but a more muddy color. Gray neck without a strong pattern. Only a few have the reddish patch.

Red-throated Loon
Gavia stellata   irW

L 25" The smallest loon, with a slender slightly upturned bill. In nonbreeding plumage, face and neck are white, with white speckling on its dark back. These star-like speckles led to the scientific name ***stellata***. The breeding adult has a gray head and neck with a patch which can look black from a distance. Coastal in winter but occurring occasionally inland, sometimes on small ponds. The only loon that can take flight from a confined space.

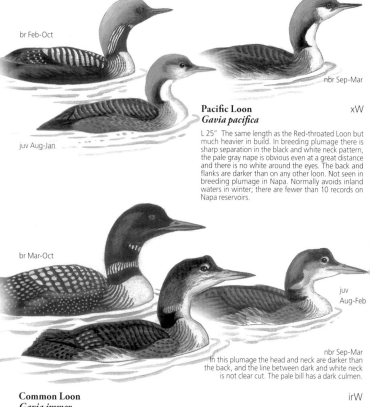

br Feb-Oct

nbr Sep-Mar

Pacific Loon
Gavia pacifica   xW

juv Aug-Jan

L 25" The same length as the Red-throated Loon but much heavier in build. In breeding plumage there is sharp separation in the black and white neck pattern, the pale gray nape is obvious even at a great distance and there is no white around the eyes. The back and flanks are darker than on any other loon. Not seen in breeding plumage in Napa. Normally avoids inland waters in winter; there are fewer than 10 records on Napa reservoirs.

br Mar-Oct

juv Aug-Feb

nbr Sep-Mar
In this plumage the head and neck are darker than the back, and the line between dark and white neck is not clear cut. The pale bill has a dark culmen.

Common Loon
Gavia immer   irW

L 32" The largest and most likely loon to be seen in Napa County. Most observations are from Lake Hennessey and Lake Berryessa but can occur on any large open water. Usually seen singly after winter storms. An uncommon spring migrant, by which time they are in bright breeding dress with jet black head and bill, snowy white breast and extensive white checkering on its black back. Look carefully when identifying a loon. Cormorants look very similar on water but have a less rounded breast and a sloping rear end.

- **Cormorants** *Phalacrocoracidae*
1 sp. Large, long-necked, blackish waterbirds.

Frequently seen wing spread posture

sloping

nbr

Cormorants swim with head at marked upward angle and sloping rear end. Dive for fish from surface. Fly with regular wingbeats, often low over water but can sail high in the air.

juv

Double-crested Cormorant
Phalacrocorax auritus

cW
luS

L 33" **Habitat:** Clear open water. Nests at Lake Hennessey in foothill pines, and at the Napa Marsh in dead eucalyptus.

Found throughout the county on ponds, lakes and reservoirs, usually seen flying singly or in flocks over land to the next pond. Historically, breeding has been recorded along the Napa River. Cormorants are not much loved by fishermen but the bulk of their food is fish of no commercial value and they make a valuable contribution toward a healthy fish population. The birds cannot waterproof their feathers like other waterbirds, so must spread their wings and tail to dry, as shown above.

br tufts are not always white

Horny knob disappears after breeding season.

- **Pelicans** *Pelecanidae*
2 sp. Huge birds, long-billed with a large pouch. Majestic in flight, flapping, gliding, soaring with neck retracted, often in formation.

American White Pelican
Pelecanus erythrorhynchos

rW, fT, lS

L 62" Forage mainly on shallow water in the marshes in small groups of about a dozen birds. Swim buoyantly; often fish close together in a line driving the fish into shallow water where they can scoop them up in their pouches. Main food consists of large and small fish of non-game species. At low tide they rest between feeding, often in large flocks on sandbars, never in trees as do Cormorants (see p. 114, **Brown Pelican**, which has a different lifestyle).

ad nbr
Sep-Feb

21

juv

American Bittern

Great Blue Heron

ad

Egrets and Herons are often seen in this hunched posture standing motionless

Black

Snowy Egret
br Feb-Jul

yellow feet

black feet and legs

Great Egret
br Feb-Jul

ad

juv Jul-Feb

Black-crowned Night Heron
Change their plumage gradually over 3 years to full ad. plumage. In top br. period the legs of some individuals are pinkish.

● Herons *Ardeidae* 7 sp. Large to medium-sized wading birds with long legs, neck and bill. Well adapted to feed in shallow water. Wings broad and rounded. Flight slow with neck retracted and trailing legs. During breeding season some have elongated head and wing plumages.

Usually hidden in dense vegetation but feeds on open mud banks, in wet meadows and even on fairly dry grassland. Mainly crepuscular but can be nocturnal. Food includes fish, frogs, salamanders, crayfish, mice and insects. Voice–a pumping slow and loud 'oong-Ka choonk'.

American Bittern   lxPt
Botaurus lentiginosus

L 28" Marshes and bogs with fresh or brackish water. Prefers good cover like reed-beds, dense tall grass or other similar vegetation.

The largest, most widespread and familiar heron. Often seen in roadside meadows, singly or in small groups, standing separately, waiting for prey. Besides fish and frogs, they hunt all sorts of vertebrates: rodents, large insects and small young birds. Adults have yellow bills, are often very pale in color and have two black plumes behind their black head stripe. Juvs. are a duller gray and have a dark crown and bicolored bill.

Great Blue Heron   cP
Ardea herodias

L 46" **Habitat:** All open habitats, from stream and pond edges, marshes, wet meadows, grassland to cultivated fields often away from water. Nests in colonies in tall trees, often over water, such as the pines at Lake Hennessey but also in eucalyptus on dry ground. The rookeries in Napa are quite small. Seldom mixes with other species.

A large, elegant, very long-necked, snowy white heron with a bright yellow bill, mostly seen singly along the margins of a lake or marsh. At sunset singles or small groups fly toward their communal roosts in trees. Previously hunted for their long nuptial plumes called aigrettes. Nearly extinct, they have now recovered in most states and are considered common. Their main food is frogs and fish but they will take any aquatic animal life.

Great Egret   cW, xS
Ardea alba

L 39" **Habitat:** All kinds of wetlands, salt and freshwater marshes, flood plains, lake shores. Occasionally hunts on dry land. Nests in trees or tall bushes near water in mixed colonies, such as the rookery at Napa State Hospital.

Only half the size of the Great but the most beautiful of all Napa herons with its long aigrettes on head, breast and back during breeding season. The black legs, yellow feet, and yellow lores are diagnostic. Very active when catching fish or tadpoles in shallow water.

Snowy Egret   cW, xS
Egretta thula

L 24" **Habitat:** Same as the Great Egret but they hunt more often on wet or even dry meadows and fields. For security, nests are built in trees near water, though the only rookery in Napa County is one mile from the river and five miles from the marshes. Secure fences make it nearly predator free.

imm

ad Green Heron

Green Heron   uW, fS
Butorides virescens

L 18" **Habitat:** Common and widely distributed. All wooded freshwater habitats have a pair. Nests and roosts alone in trees and bushes with dense foliage.

Small, chunky, dark-colored, broad-winged and short-legged. Does not resemble a heron when seen crouching in the shadow of a wooded bank waiting for fish to swim by, nor when stalking prey with great patience in shallow water. Secretive and solitary in all its habits, often overlooked before being seen flying away low over the water. Call is a sharp, harsh explosive 'skyow.'

Sleeps all day, often in large roosts, hunched up and hidden in treetops. At sunset, flies out to feeding grounds and hunts, usually alone. Young birds in dull brown colors fly with rather fast wingbeats and can be mistaken for a large owl. I heard their hollow 'quack' several times at night as they flew over the city of Napa.

Black-crowned Night Heron   uP
Nycticorax nycticorax

L 25" **Habitat:** Varied. Feeds in all kinds of wetlands, fresh or saltwater. Needs large trees nearby for roosting and nesting. Often in large colonies. The largest Napa rookery with nearly 150 nests at the State Hospital is not close to water.

● **Geese, Swans and Ducks** *Anatidae* 34 sp. Long-necked, web-footed waterbirds. Well-represented in Napa with 10 breeding (possibly + 2), 23 wintering and 1 introduced sp., which also breeds.

Tundra Swan

White-fronted

Snow Goose

Brant

Canada Goose

Mallard p. 26

Cackling

Cackling *minima*

Cackling *taverneri*

Canada *moffitii*

Brant *Branta bernicla*   xTs

L 24" Very small, dark goose, the only one with a totally black head, lacking the white cheeks of the Cackler, which they otherwise resemble. Their flight is rapid and agile.

Some ducks are similar in size but none look as dark in flight as a Brant or Cackler with completely black wings. All the ducks have longer necks and bills, which are clearly visible, even in flight.

Cackling Goose *Branta hutchinsii*   irW

L 22"-32" A dwarf replica of the Canada, with a doll-like face and high-pitched cackling call. Small flocks of ***B.h. minima*** winter annually on the Napa River floodplain. The **'Aleutian' Cackling Goose**, ***B.h. leucopareia*** is expanding its winter range to include the river floodplain. Other relatively small subspecies of both Canada and Cackling Goose are seen more regularly in all different habitats.

It was only in 2004 that the Cackling and Canada Geese were recognized as separate species. The identification of the smallest darker Cacklers and the larger breeding pale Canadas is easy but some winter visitors are between them in size. Cacklers usually have a smaller, shorter bill but identification of intermediates remains a problem.

Canada Goose   cW, fS
Branta canadensis

L 34"-44" **Habitat**: Breeds on farm ponds, reservoirs and around the larger lakes, along the Napa River and in the marshes. Need meadows nearby for grazing.

Once a winter visitor, the subspecies, ***B.c. moffitii***, is widespread and an early breeder. Before the visitors leave for their northern breeding haunts in Mar., the first pairs start to lay. Very adaptable and tolerant of human presence. The breeding population has reached its limit because breeding pairs are rather aggressive toward their neighbors and there is a shortage of nesting space.

Tule Goose lrW
A.a.gambelli

The entire population of this larger subspecies of the Greater White-fronted Goose winters in the Sacramento Valley. It could occur in Napa, however identification is difficult. The Tule Goose is more often found in marshes than open fields.

juv

ad

Greater White-fronted Goose
Anser albifrons uW

L 28" A rare annual winter visitor. Mainly seen grazing on farmland, meadows or marshes, in the company of wintering Canada Geese. Their lighter build, white face contrasting with the brown head, pink bill and orange feet distinguish them from the larger, clumsy domestic geese. There are some introduced Greylags that remain on farm ponds all year round and breed.

juv Aug-Jan

Ross's Goose xV
Chen rossii

L 23" This small, short-billed goose is a very rare winter visitor.

Snow Goose rW
Chen caerulescens

L 28" Rare winter visitor. All white but sometimes yellowish stains on their heads. The black primaries are best seen in flight (see opposite page). Until January, young birds have a variably gray head and neck. The dark-colored, white-headed variant called Blue Goose has not yet been recorded in Napa County.

ad

ad

The small yellow spot on the lores, in front of the eyes, varies greatly in size, and is missing in some individuals.

Can only see the full size and massive body of these huge birds when they are standing.

Tundra Swan irW
Cygnus columbianus

L 52" A rare, visitor from the far north, not observed every year in the county. Usually in freshwater reservoirs, lakes or after heavy rain on flooded fields. Can be seen in small groups of 2-3, grazing on grain fields or standing, i.e. roosting in very shallow water. A large and splendid bird, all white with a black bill.

juv Aug-Mar
In their first plumage, they look dirty white with blotches, becoming all white in their second year while still retaining some gray on head and neck until mid-winter.

25

juv

♂ nbr

♂ br

Wood Duck
Aix sponsa

rP

L 18" **Habitat**: Freshwater ponds, reservoirs and streams with well-sheltered overhanging vegetation and large trees nearby for nesting. They accept nest boxes.

Only the protection and restoration of the right habitat will assure the future of the most colorful duck in the county. Nest boxes are a great help but not enough. Wood Ducks also need shallow, undisturbed, rich streams and similar freshwater refuges. Rather shy in the wild.

angled line on base of bill

broad eye patch

dark nail

♀

smaller spotting on flanks

grayish, short

straight line on base of bill

narrow eye ring

pale nail

♀

larger pale spotting on flanks

mustard color, longer

♀ **Wood Duck**: dark head with some gloss on crown, broad white ring around eye, dark back with glossy wing coverts, longer body and tail, short legs.

♀ **Mandarin Duck**: pale, ash gray head with narrow eye patch and longer eye stripe. Paler all over, shorter body and tail, longer legs. Eclipse ♂ is similar.

Mandarin Duck
Aix galericulata

escaped

L 17" Some escapees have been recorded in Napa from the feral flock of several hundred in Sonoma County, northwest of Calistoga. They may compete for nesting sites with the Wood Duck but cannot hybridize with them.

♂ br

♀

♂ nbr similar greenish bill, darker breast

♂ br
Oct-May

silvery gray

black

♂ br
Sep-May

Mallard
Anas platyrhynchos

cW, fS

L 23" **Habitat**: Most adaptable of all ducks. Unusual to find even a tiny pond with vegetation cover without a nesting pair. Found in more open and brackish water in winter.

The most familiar of all water fowl. Males in br.. plumage are easy to identify. Females can be confused with other dabbling ducks. Look for details. Wild birds are shy and retiring but adapt quickly to human presence and can become quite tame. This is the ancestor of all domestic duck varieties except the Muscovys, of which ferals can be observed anywhere.

Gadwall
Anas strepera

cW, luS

L 20" **Habitat**: Freshwater ponds, lakes, wetlands and marshes with thick vegetation. Winters on open, fresh or brackish water.

Nearly always seen in pairs that remain together amongst the wintering flocks. The pair bond is established in late summer and pairs remain together through the following spring. The rather drab gray male is easily distinguished by his black rear end. Females are smaller, more mottled and also grayer than female Mallards, with a steep forehead and plain face.

♀ Shoveler

♂ nbr Shoveler

Mallard ♂ nbr

Wood Duck

♂ nbr Eurasian Wigeon

Gadwall ♂ nbr

♀

♂ nbr American Wigeon

♀

♂ br Oct-Jun

♂ br

♂ br Hybrid American x Eurasian Wigeon

♀

eclipse ♂

♂ br Nov-Jun

Dabbling Ducks in flight: Males with bright colors and distinctive patterns are easily recognized. Females are easier to identify in flight because the speculum shows up as a broad wingbar.

Shoveler: ♂ dark belly, blue-gray forewing and heavy bill
Mallard: large size, brown belly, violet blue speculum with white borders
American Wigeon: rounded body, pointed tail, white belly, large white shoulder patch
Eurasian Wigeon: similar, brown head, looks darker
Gadwall: white belly, square white speculum visible above and below
Wood Duck: very dark with pale belly and long tail

Note:
Ducks fly fast, so you need experience to identify them.

American Wigeon   cW
Anas americana
L 20" A very common winter visitor, seen mostly in marshes on fresh and brackish water but also on large lakes, and in saltwater. Some might stay all year but nesting in Napa is unlikely for this northern breeder.

Flies fast, often in dense flocks, wheeling and turning in perfect unison, like teal. Frequently seen grazing in fields like geese, for which their short bills are well adapted. Also sifts plants from water's surface. The old name 'Baldpate' describes the male well with his pale forehead and crown. The female's rounded and grayish head is her best field mark.

American x Eurasian Wigeon
Where their breeding ranges overlap, American and Eurasian Wigeon occasionally interbreed. The bright males of such liaisons are variable but easily identified. Identification of the drab females is difficult.

Eurasian Wigeon   rW
Anas penelope
L 20" Most common in coastal waters, rare in Napa and usually seen in flocks of 'Baldpates.' Once very rare but now seen regularly. This may indicate that birdwatchers are now more observant. It's possible that some breed in the far north. Males are easy to distinguish from American but the females are only more gray and uniform in color.

Northern Shoveler   cW, lxs
Anas clypeata

L 19" **Habitat**: Shallow, stagnant fresh-water. A common winter visitor in the marshes. A few pairs breed annually in the wet grassland.

Both sexes are recognized easily by their heavy spoon-shaped bills, held downwards when swimming. The male's strikingly patterned plumage is visible at a great distance. The bright white breast, dark head and rufous flanks are unique. Small groups feed together, milling around, scooping plankton from the water's surface. Seldom tips-up like Mallards or Pintails. Flight is fast, erratic, with sudden downward plunges, resembling teal.

27

Blue-winged Teal — xS
Anas discors — nb

L 15½" **Habitat**: Small, shallow marshy ponds. Also found on mudflats with other ducks during spring and fall migrations.

The most abundant small duck in the interior of North America but a rare spring and fall migrant along the West Coast. In recent years seen more frequently in Napa. Some stay in winter and a few remain throughout the year. There is a single county breeding record. Males can be distinguished by white crescents on their faces and white femoral patches toward their black rear.

Blue-wings and Cinnamons are very closely related and sometimes hybridize. The male offspring are variable and can be confused with molting males of either species.

♀ **Blue-winged**: Similar to female Cinnamon, but overall more gray. Larger paler patch at base of shorter bill. In flight, the pale blue wing-patch is obvious.

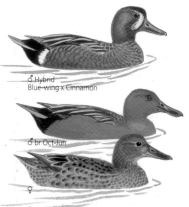

♂ Hybrid
Blue-wing x Cinnamon

♂ br Oct-Jun

Cinnamon Teal — uW,
Anas cyanoptera — lus

L 16" **Habitat**: Fresh and brackish water wetlands, most common in marshes, on mudbanks with dense vegetation and also on the northern most point of Lake Berryessa.

In late fall, there are rare sightings when migrating birds pass swiftly en route to southern winter quarters. Cinnamons often concentrate in large numbers during spring migration, from mid-Jan., building up to Mar., on their way to their northern breeding haunts. A few birds stay to nest from Apr. onwards in dense perennial vegetation near freshwater. Bright chestnut-colored males, with gray-blue wing patches only seen in flight, are unique.

♀ **Cinnamon**: Similar to a Blue wing female but plainer, and overall brown with a less distinctive face patch. The longish bill can give them a shoveler-like appearance.

♂

♂ br
Oct-Jun

All ducks have their particular courtship display, especially when pairing up. They achieve the most peculiar postures, such as this example of the Green-winged teal. Males often court in groups when females are not present. This can be easily observed, since they usually court on open water.

♂ nbr Jul-Sep

♀ **Green-winged**: Compact with a much shorter, slender bill than other female Teals. Dark-colored with a prominent, pale streak on her tail. The nbr. ♀ is very similar.

♂ br
Oct-Jun

Green-winged Teal — cW
Anas crecca

L 14" Tiny, agile but hardy duck. Arrives in large numbers during late fall, stays throughout winter, and the last leave at the end of Apr. A few may remain but nesting is unlikely for this far-northern breeder. Usually forages in small groups but can gather in marshes in flocks of hundreds. Prefers shallow waters, channels and mudflats with tall grasses and sedges growing at the water's edge, where they can hide and rest. Mainly a seed-eater, often visits grain fields but also scoops small crustacea and aquatic plants from the water's surface.

Intermediate males with both breast and scapular stripes are quite possibly aberrant Green-wings and not hybrids.

Eurasian Teal: This subspecies, which possibly breeds in Alaska, has not yet been recorded in Napa but could occur one day. It's like a Green-wing with a white horizontal scapular stripe.

♀ Mallard p. 26

♀ Gadwall p. 26

♂ Blue-winged Teal

♀ Wigeon p. 27

♀ Green-winged Teal

♂

♀ Shoveler p. 27

♀

♂ Cinnamon Teal

♀ Northern Pintail

The Mallard is larger than other ducks and flies more slowly. Look for size, shape and wing pattern as well as belly color.

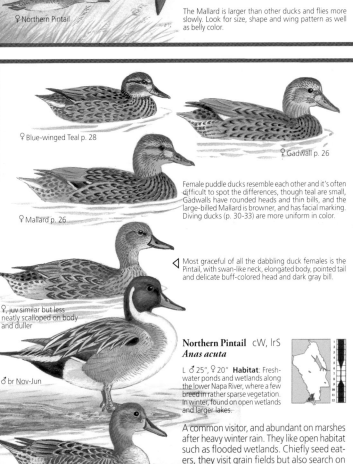

♀ Blue-winged Teal p. 28

♀ Gadwall p. 26

♀ Mallard p. 26

Female puddle ducks resemble each other and it's often difficult to spot the differences, though teal are small, Gadwalls have rounded heads and thin bills, and the large-billed Mallard is browner, and has facial marking. Diving ducks (p. 30-33) are more uniform in color.

◁ Most graceful of all the dabbling duck females is the Pintail, with swan-like neck, elongated body, pointed tail and delicate buff-colored head and dark gray bill.

♀, juv similar but less neatly scalloped on body and duller

♂ br Nov-Jun

Northern Pintail cW, lrS
Anas acuta

L ♂25", ♀20" **Habitat**: Freshwater ponds and wetlands along the lower Napa River, where a few breed in rather sparse vegetation. In winter, found on open wetlands and larger lakes.

A common visitor, and abundant on marshes after heavy winter rain. They like open habitat such as flooded wetlands. Chiefly seed eaters, they visit grain fields but also search on tidal mudflats for aquatic life such as snails, crabs and insects. Usually very wary and hard to approach. Among ducks, they are the fastest fliers and the easiest to identify. The male is quite pale with a black rear, snowy white breast and chocolate head. They pair up before the spring exodus. Their communal courtship display is spectacular.

♂ nbr Jul-Oct

The best field mark for both sexes in all plumages is their elegant line with long body, neck, bill and tail. In eclipse the male's bill remains blue-black while the female's is gray.

Diving and Sea Ducks: Most ducks on the Napa list belong to this mixed group. There are 16 diving, compared with 11 dabbling ducks (p. 26-29). With legs set farther back, they are good swimmers and divers, and feed deep underwater. They walk awkwardly and need a long runway from which to take flight. 'Divers' are shorter-necked and more compact than dabblers. The Ruddy is almost helpless on land and the mergansers are specialized fishers.

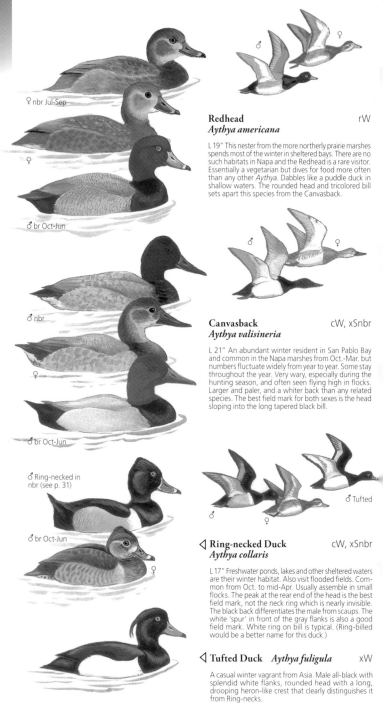

♀ nbr Jul-Sep

♀

♂ br Oct-Jun

Redhead rW
Aythya americana

L 19" This nester from the more northerly prairie marshes spends most of the winter in sheltered bays. There are no such habitats in Napa and the Redhead is a rare visitor. Essentially a vegetarian but dives for food more often than any other *Aythya*. Dabbles like a puddle duck in shallow waters. The rounded head and tricolored bill sets apart this species from the Canvasback.

♂ nbr

♀

♂ br Oct-Jun

Canvasback cW, xSnbr
Aythya valisineria

L 21" An abundant winter resident in San Pablo Bay and common in the Napa marshes from Oct.-Mar. but numbers fluctuate widely from year to year. Some stay throughout the year. Very wary, especially during the hunting season, and often seen flying high in flocks. Larger and paler, and a whiter back than any related species. The best field mark for both sexes is the head sloping into the long tapered black bill.

♂ Ring-necked in nbr (see p. 31)

♂ Tufted

♂

♀

♂ br Oct-Jun

♀

◁ Ring-necked Duck cW, xSnbr
Aythya collaris

L 17" Freshwater ponds, lakes and other sheltered waters are their winter habitat. Also visit flooded fields. Common from Oct. to mid-Apr. Usually assemble in small flocks. The peak at the rear end of the head is the best field mark, not the neck ring which is nearly invisible. The black back differentiates the male from scaups. The white 'spur' in front of the gray flanks is also a good field mark. White ring on bill is typical. (Ring-billed would be a better name for this duck.)

◁ Tufted Duck *Aythya fuligula* xW

A casual winter vagrant from Asia. Male all-black with splendid white flanks, rounded head with a long, drooping heron-like crest that clearly distinguishes it from Ring-necks.

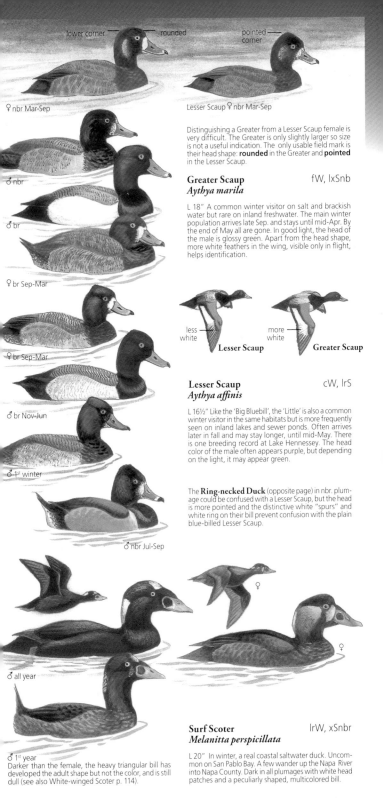

lower corner — rounded   pointed — corner

♀ nbr Mar-Sep

Lesser Scaup ♀ nbr Mar-Sep

Distinguishing a Greater from a Lesser Scaup female is very difficult. The Greater is only slightly larger so size is not a useful indication. The only usable field mark is their head shape: **rounded** in the Greater and **pointed** in the Lesser Scaup.

Greater Scaup   fW, lxSnb
Aythya marila

L 18" A common winter visitor on salt and brackish water but rare on inland freshwater. The main winter population arrives late Sep. and stays until mid-Apr. By the end of May all are gone. In good light, the head of the male is glossy green. Apart from the head shape, more white feathers in the wing, visible only in flight, helps identification.

♂ nbr

♂ br

♀ br Sep-Mar

♀ br Sep-Mar

less white   **Lesser Scaup**   more white   **Greater Scaup**

Lesser Scaup   cW, lrS
Aythya affinis

L 16½" Like the 'Big Bluebill', the 'Little' is also a common winter visitor in the same habitats but is more frequently seen on inland lakes and sewer ponds. Often arrives later in fall and may stay longer, until mid-May. There is one breeding record at Lake Hennessey. The head color of the male often appears purple, but depending on the light, it may appear green.

♂ br Nov-Jun

♂ 1st winter

The **Ring-necked Duck** (opposite page) in nbr. plumage could be confused with a Lesser Scaup, but the head is more pointed and the distinctive white "spurs" and white ring on their bill prevent confusion with the plain blue-billed Lesser Scaup.

♂ nbr Jul-Sep

♂ all year

Surf Scoter   lrW, xSnbr
Melanitta perspicillata

L 20" In winter, a real coastal saltwater duck. Uncommon on San Pablo Bay. A few wander up the Napa River into Napa County. Dark in all plumages with white head patches and a peculiarly shaped, multicolored bill.

♂ 1st year
Darker than the female, the heavy triangular bill has developed the adult shape but not the color, and is still dull (see also White-winged Scoter p. 114).

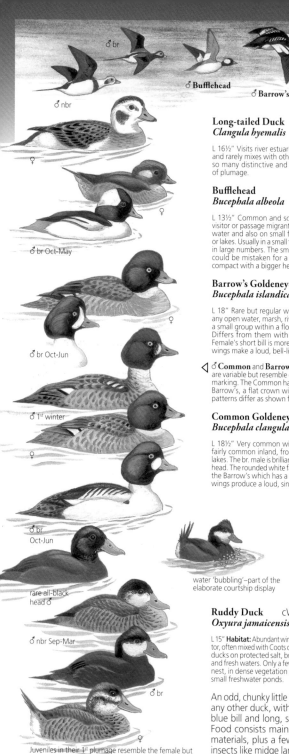

♂ br

♂ nbr

♂ Bufflehead

♂ Barrow's

♂ Common Goldeneye

♀

♀ br Oct-May

♀

♂ br Oct-Jun

♂ 1st winter

♀

♂ br Oct-Jun

rare all-black head ♂

♂ nbr Sep-Mar

♂ br

Juveniles in their 1st plumage resemble the female but with a cheek patch more like a nbr male, and only a faint shadow-like facial stripe. The parents molt at about the time the brood is half grown, at which time they abandon the young.

Long-tailed Duck ixTSnbr
Clangula hyemalis

L 16½" Visits river estuaries in small groups or singly, and rarely mixes with other ducks. No other duck has so many distinctive and complex seasonal changes of plumage.

Bufflehead cW, xSnbr
Bucephala albeola

L 13½" Common and some years abundant winter visitor or passage migrant, found on salt and brackish water and also on small freshwater ponds, reservoirs or lakes. Usually in a small flock, they sometimes gather in large numbers. The smallest North American duck, could be mistaken for a Horned Grebe but is more compact with a bigger head.

Barrow's Goldeneye xW
Bucephala islandica

L 18" Rare but regular winter visitor. Could occur on any open water, marsh, river or lake. Usually singles or a small group within a flock of Common Goldeneyes. Differs from them with a rounder, bulbous head. Female's short bill is more yellow. In flight (see above) wings make a loud, bell-like whistling sound.

◁ ♂ **Common** and **Barrow's** in their 1st winter plumage are variable but resemble each other in color and head marking. The Common has a slightly peaked head, the Barrow's, a flat crown with mane. In flight, the wing patterns differ as shown for adults (see above).

Common Goldeneye fW, lxSnbr
Bucephala clangula

L 18½" Very common winter visitor in marshes, and fairly common inland, from farm and sewer ponds to lakes. The br. male is brilliant white with a green peaked head. The rounded white face patch separates him from the Barrow's which has a crescent patch. In flight, the wings produce a loud, singing metallic sound.

water 'bubbling'–part of the elaborate courtship display

rapid flight with buzzing wingbeats

Ruddy Duck cW, xS
Oxyura jamaicensis

L 15" **Habitat:** Abundant winter visitor, often mixed with Coots or other ducks on protected salt, brackish and fresh waters. Only a few pairs nest, in dense vegetation beside small freshwater ponds.

An odd, chunky little duck. So different from any other duck, with his big head, swollen blue bill and long, spiky, often raised tail. Food consists mainly of seeds and plant materials, plus a few soft-bodied aquatic insects like midge larvae, mostly caught by diving. Never on land since they can hardly walk. Unlike other ducks, the male assists in rearing the brood.

While the female incubates, the males group together to molt. They don't help the female raise the brood.

For nesting, Mergansers need mature trees with cavities such as Pileated Woodpecker holes.

♂ br Nov-Jul

♂ nbr Jul-Oct are like ♀, but retain the extensive white on wing—only seen in flight. Juv have pale face marking and smaller crest.

Common Merganser
Mergus merganser

uW, xS

♀

L 25" **Habitat:** In winter, uncommon on lower Napa River, reservoirs, sewer ponds and lakes. Breeding is restricted because the swift-flowing wooded streams needed are lacking in Napa. The brood is led downstream and reared on larger quiet waters.

In silhouette and habits they resemble a Cormorant more than they do a duck. Feeding habits are similar. To locate fish, their main food, they often swim with their head half underwater. Also take crayfish, frogs, salamanders and water insects. Often seen resting on a gravel or sandbank.

← crest at times erect

♀

♀

♂

♂ br Nov-May

Red-breasted Merganser
Mergus serrator

xW

L 23" More often on saltwater than inland. Male's brown breast divided by a white collar from the black double-crested head is diagnostic. It's more difficult to separate the females. Looks more spindly than the larger Common Merganser, head more loosely crested and paler red.

♂ nbr May-Oct
Diffuse white chin, in flight larger white wing patch than ♀. Red-breasts have thinner bills than Commons.

← raised crest folded →

♂ br
Sep-Jun

♂

♀

Hooded Merganser
Lophodytes cucullatus

uW

L 18" Uncommon winter visitor on sheltered fresh and brackish waters. Male, unmistakable. Females and young, rather dark, drab little ducks with long tails. Like all mergansers, very fast and direct in flight, often in small, compact flocks.

♂ nbr Jul-Sep
Like ♀ with totally dark bill. Both have frosty-brown loose crests. With crests folded, could be confused with the shorter billed Bufflehead ♀.

The 'sanitary brigade' will gather around small carrion to clear it up. Crows and Ravens will join in.

juv

ad

● **New World Vultures** *Cathartidae* 1 sp. New World vultures and condors are modified *Ciconiidaes* and are not closely related to eagles or Old World vultures. They have no voice and, except for a soft hissing, are generally silent like storks (see also p. 115, **California Condor**).

Turkey Vulture
Cathartes aura

cP

L 26" **Habitat**: Seen everywhere, usually soaring high overhead. Prefer open country and woodland. Need tall trees for resting and hollow logs for nesting.

You cannot be in Napa without seeing a TV, as they are called. Highly gregarious. Roosts in isolated trees or cliffs; nests in hollow logs, rocky mountain outcrops and at daybreak are often seen in tall dead trees waiting for the warmth of the sun. Most search for food alone over vast areas, often along highways. Watching one another, they can gather in large numbers when carrion is found.

ad
see also p. 42

juv

ad

● **Osprey** *Pandionidae* 1 sp. Only one species in this family and one of the few birds found on all continents except Antarctica. Highly specialized in catching fish. After hovering it dives feet first into the water. Feet and talons very strong.

Osprey
Pandion haliaetus

rP

L 23" **Habitat**: Clear and calm water with surface-feeding fish, as at Lakes Hennessey, Berryessa and Curry, and also deep pools along Napa River.

After decline due to pesticides, they are now recovering. A regular resident in Napa County, often known as the Fish Eagle. Their bulky nests, to which they add more material each year, are now a common sight. They nest in living or dead trees, and readily accept manmade structures, as at Lake Berryessa.

● **Diurnal Raptors** *Accipitridae* 12 sp. **Hawks, Kites** and **Eagles** all belong to this well-represented family. Sexes usually alike, but females larger than males. Immature plumages often confusing. Most are powerful hunters. The smallest, only 11" long, weighs 5 oz., the largest 30", weighs 10 lbs., with a wingspan of 80" (see p. 41-43 in flight).

uW, rS **Golden Eagle**
Aquila chrysaetos

L 30" **Habitat:** Mountain and ranch country with open wooded areas and grassland. Nests in big trees, mostly pines, or on cliffs.

Seen alone or in pairs. A magnificent, powerful hunter. Juveniles are not easily distinguished from young Bald Eagles. At Lake Berryessa I saw them soaring together. The Golden's head is slightly smaller, more elegant, the tail a bit longer, but this is not always clearly visible. Their body is totally dark, not patchy as with the young Bald Eagle. They show the golden color on their nape at every age.

rW, xS **Bald Eagle**
Haliaetus leucocephalus

L 31" **Habitat:** Lakes Berryessa and Hennessey, where a few nest in tall pine trees. In winter, short stays in the marshes.

In recent decades eagles were found wintering at the larger county reservoirs. The breeding population has grown slowly since the first successful nest at Lake Berryessa in 1992. Some juvenile northern California eagles are known to migrate to southeastern Alaska during their first fall and winter, returning the following spring. Adult birds are easy to identify with their white head and tail but not so the immatures (see under **Golden Eagle** above, and also p. 42).

Normally seen in pairs, but in winter they gather in communal roosts at sunset, arriving from all directions. Up to 50 birds have been observed at one roost in the marshes on Knight Island.

White-tailed Kite
Elanus leucurus

uP

L 15" **Habitat**: In the valley and tidal district grassland and meadows, with trees and tall bushes nearby where there is an abundance of small rodents, such as jumping mice, their main food.

The most graceful raptor. Perches at treetop level on an exposed dead branch. They nest in oaks and build a deep stick nest that is large for their size. They defend it fiercely against any intruder, even those larger than themselves. The male often demonstrates his acrobatic courtship flight. Their voice is a short, harsh whistling note and they are noisy during the breeding season.

Falcon-like with longish tail and pointed wings. Soars over grassland, hovers for a moment before pouncing on a mouse. They hunt throughout the day, but are most active at dusk.

From above juv.. and females are similar, brown with an obvious white rump.
From below the juv.. looks more colorful with its 'orange' breast and dark brown head.

Harriers fly gracefully, low over ground to hunt, turning and twisting, looking for prey. Take mostly rodents, frogs, snakes, some birds, large insects and even fish.

Northern Harrier
Circus cyaneus

uW, lrs

L 18" **Habitat**: Open farm and grassland, marshes. Perches on low fenceposts, seldom on trees, mostly on the ground, where they also build their nest.

The male's gull-like colors, long wings, long tail and owl-like facial disk separates the harrier from all other raptors. In spring males put on a spectacular aerial display. Flying upwards, calling loudly 'check-ek-ek-ek-ek,' making a final upturn, a stall, followed by a dive. Nesting on the ground, they are vulnerable to all sorts of disturbances. Few nest successfully in the county, although there are many potential habitats. (They may benefit when the marshes are restored to a more natural condition.)

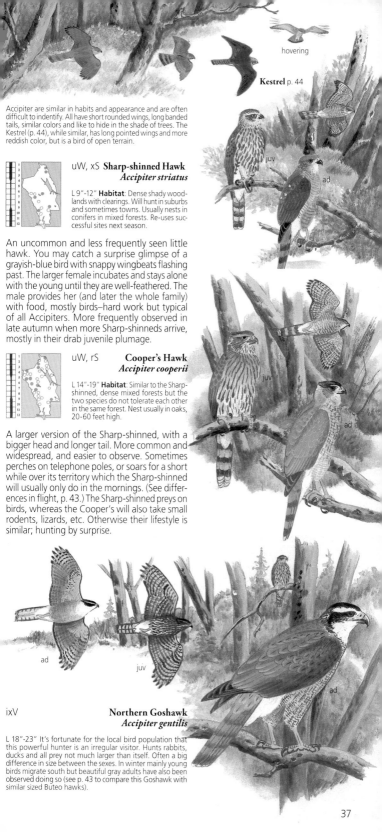

hovering

Kestrel p. 44

Accipiter are similar in habits and appearance and are often difficult to indentify. All have short rounded wings, long banded tails, similar colors and like to hide in the shade of trees. The Kestrel (p. 44), while similar, has long pointed wings and more reddish color, but is a bird of open terrain.

juv

ad

uW, xS **Sharp-shinned Hawk**
Accipiter striatus

L 9"-12" **Habitat**: Dense shady woodlands with clearings. Will hunt in suburbs and sometimes towns. Usually nests in conifers in mixed forests. Re-uses successful sites next season.

An uncommon and less frequently seen little hawk. You may catch a surprise glimpse of a grayish-blue bird with snappy wingbeats flashing past. The larger female incubates and stays alone with the young until they are well-feathered. The male provides her (and later the whole family) with food, mostly birds–hard work but typical of all Accipiters. More frequently observed in late autumn when more Sharp-shinneds arrive, mostly in their drab juvenile plumage.

uW, rS **Cooper's Hawk**
Accipiter cooperii

L 14"-19" **Habitat**: Similar to the Sharp-shinned, dense mixed forests but the two species do not tolerate each other in the same forest. Nest usually in oaks, 20-60 feet high.

juv

ad

A larger version of the Sharp-shinned, with a bigger head and longer tail. More common and widespread, and easier to observe. Sometimes perches on telephone poles, or soars for a short while over its territory which the Sharp-shinned will usually only do in the mornings. (See differences in flight, p. 43.) The Sharp-shinned preys on birds, whereas the Cooper's will also take small rodents, lizards, etc. Otherwise their lifestyle is similar; hunting by surprise.

ad

juv

ad

ixV **Northern Goshawk**
Accipiter gentilis

L 18"-23" It's fortunate for the local bird population that this powerful hunter is an irregular visitor. Hunts rabbits, ducks and all prey not much larger than itself. Often a big difference in size between the sexes. In winter mainly young birds migrate south but beautiful gray adults have also been observed doing so (see p. 43 to compare this Goshawk with similar sized Buteo hawks).

37

Red-shouldered Hawk
Buteo lineatus fP

L 17" **Habitat**: Wet woodland along Napa River and nearby forested upland. Frequently seen along highways and roads in the valley, as well as in towns. Nests in large trees, including eucalyptus.

A sluggish bird except in flight, when it's very playful. Its short rounded wings and long tail always remind me of an Accipiter hawk. The rufous body, underwing coverts and broad banded tail are quite flashy.

For a raptor, this small Buteo is colorful with bright rufous underparts, white-banded dark wings, 'red' shoulders and barred black and white tails (for juv. see p. 40). There are no different color morphs as with the other four Buteos in Napa. Commonly seen perched on telephone cables along the highways. You can observe them in and around the city of Napa and during spring courtship hear their repeated loud, clear and high-pitched scream, 'Kee aaah, Kee aaah.'

light

long narrow wings

pointed

long

dark

long

always pale

Typically for most Buteos, independently of sex or age, there are different color morphs: a common light, with white underside and contrasting rusty breast, a chocolate brown and also an intermediate morph (juveniles are different, see p. 40).

Swainson's Hawk
Buteo swainsoni xS

L 19" **Habitat**: Open grassland country, with some large trees where they rest, and build their bulky nest.

Compared to the heavily built Red-tail, this is a slim, elegant Buteo, more like a slender-headed large Kite. In flight, the long pointed wings and long tail are distinctive, and the wings are raised in a shallow V, resembling a Harrier. During field work for this book, the first Napa County nest was discovered just south of the city of Napa. We observed five birds. Two pairs showed off their elegant aerial display. One pair flew off high in the air, in a northwesterly direction, while the other pair brought sticks to their nest.

Harlan's Hawk In 1830 Audubon described this hawk as a distinct species. Now it's included in the Red-tailed subspecies complex. Variable in color but never has a red tail. Not yet officially identified in Napa but recorded in neighboring counties and could occur in Napa.

Harlan's ad

light ad

dark juv

cW, fS **Red-tailed Hawk**
Buteo jamaicensis

L 19" **Habitat**: From the marshes in the south to the open woodland ridges in the north. Nests in tall trees, dead or living, often in nearly treeless country.

This is the most common hawk in the county. Often seen day after day, perched on the same favorite dead branch, pole or fencepost along a road or highway. A stocky bird with broad shoulders, a lazy but powerful hunter, feeds mainly on small mammals such as mice, gophers, squirrels and rabbits. Also takes road-kill and carrion. Napa breeders are sedentary but in winter more birds move in from the north, and that's when you can see them everywhere.

No two Red-tails, ad. or juv., are exactly the same color. The most commonly seen in Napa is the light morph with a speckled V on the scapulars and a reddish tail. Birds in the juv.. dark morph have brown tails with fine barrings in their first year and resemble the ad. dark morph (see p. 40).

◁ dark ▷

light

see p. 41, 43

Ferruginous Hawk rW
Buteo regalis

L 23" Prefers open, treeless, grassy hillsides. A regular but rare winter visitor from the plains. Generally seen perching on the ground waiting for small mammals but also hunts from the air. Very fond of ground squirrels, it's amazing that such a large eagle-like raptor takes such small prey.

39

Buteo Hawks, lst year: Not only adults a[re] puzzling in their different color morphs. [In] their 1st year, they can look very differe[nt] from the definitive adult hawks.

Red-shouldered Hawk (p. 38)

This is the smallest hawk, compact but long-tailed, an[d] in some ways resembles a molting Cooper's Hawk. Th[e] rufous color is present but more patchy. The streake[d] breast, of one color in the adult, is typical along wi[th] the spotted rather than barred underside. Wings an[d] mantle are more brownish and mottled. Genera[l] looks a bit untidy.

Red-tailed Hawk (p. 39)

Young Red-tails are not red-tailed. They have a da[rk] grayish tail with small bandings in all color morphs. The[ir] compact shape separates them from other Buteos and [it] is the species most likely to be observed. The dark morp[h] is nearly black with some paler mottling on wing an[d] back. The commoner light birds have a dark head an[d] pale breast, dark streaked belly and perhaps a nea[r] white V on the back. Again, the overall impression [is] mottled and untidy.

Swainson's Hawk (p. 38)

The elegant shape, with long pointed wings whi[ch] reach the end of the long tail when perched, and e[s]pecially the smaller head, sets this hawk apart fro[m] other Buteos. The dark morph, normally only 10% [of] a population, always has paler undertail coverts. W[e] saw two dark and three pale morphs in Napa; one [a] young bird with heavily spotted belly. The light morp[h] has a pale head and chin. In worn plumage the be[lly] becomes paler.

Rough-legged Hawk
Buteo lagopus

A rare visitor from the north. Likes open non-woode[d] terrain and often perches on the ground. Hunts sm[all] mammals, often from a low fencepost or hoveri[ng] low over the ground like a kestrel, with low flappi[ng] wingbeats. This far south usually seen in 1st year plu[m]age with the typically dark patch on belly and broa[d] terminal band on pale tail. There is also a dark morp[h] which is very difficult to distinguish from a Red-ta[il]. Rough-leggeds always have feathered legs and sm[all] feet, not easy to see in the field (see opposite pag[e] **Ferruginous Hawk**).

'window'

banded tail — rufous

Red-shouldered Hawk
Rufous underwing coverts, short wings, pale 'window' on outer wings, long tail with narrow light bands, very playful in flight.

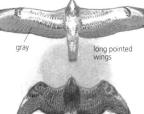

gray

long pointed wings

light

Swainson's Hawk
Narrow, slender head; long, narrow pointed wings, pale underwing coverts against dark flight feathers. Both morphs pale undertail coverts, elegant flight. (See Osprey in flight, p. 42.)

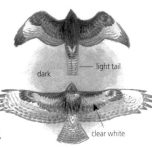

dark — light tail

clear white

Red-tailed Hawk
Big-headed; dark marks on leading edge of broad, long wings (patagial marks); square wing panels in both morphs; broad, narrow-banded, pale tail; often soars very high.

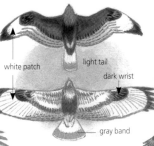

white patch

light tail

dark wrist

gray band

Rough-legged Hawk
Large white panels in flight feathers; dark, bold wrist patch; light-colored tail with gray terminal band.

clean whitish tail

Ferruginous

clean white

Ferruginous Hawk
Light morph from below, very pale, nearly white; dark morph bicolored; wings broad with narrow, pointed tips.

dark juv

light juv

Ferruginous Hawk (p. 39)
The light gray head, snowy white chin and breast, and the few dark spots on the white belly are unique. From a distance wings and back appear very dark, nearly black. The rare dark morph is less rufous than the dark adult, and has some barrings on pale tail. The large beak and strong feet give this hawk an eagle-like appearance, however its main prey, surprisingly, is small mammals (see under ad. text p. 39).

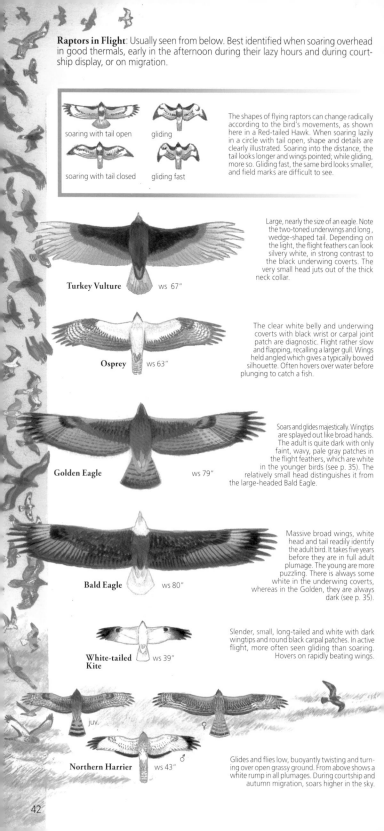

Raptors in Flight: Usually seen from below. Best identified when soaring overhead in good thermals, early in the afternoon during their lazy hours and during courtship display, or on migration.

soaring with tail open

gliding

soaring with tail closed

gliding fast

The shapes of flying raptors can change radically according to the bird's movements, as shown here in a Red-tailed Hawk. When soaring lazily in a circle with tail open, shape and details are clearly illustrated. Soaring into the distance, the tail looks longer and wings pointed; while gliding, more so. Gliding fast, the same bird looks smaller, and field marks are difficult to see.

Turkey Vulture   ws 67"

Large, nearly the size of an eagle. Note the two-toned underwings and long, wedge-shaped tail. Depending on the light, the flight feathers can look silvery white, in strong contrast to the black underwing coverts. The very small head juts out of the thick neck collar.

Osprey   ws 63"

The clear white belly and underwing coverts with black wrist or carpal joint patch are diagnostic. Flight rather slow and flapping, recalling a larger gull. Wings held angled which gives a typically bowed silhouette. Often hovers over water before plunging to catch a fish.

Golden Eagle   ws 79"

Soars and glides majestically. Wingtips are splayed out like broad hands. The adult is quite dark with only faint, wavy, pale gray patches in the flight feathers, which are white in the younger birds (see p. 35). The relatively small head distinguishes it from the large-headed Bald Eagle.

Bald Eagle   ws 80"

Massive broad wings, white head and tail readily identify the adult bird. It takes five years before they are in full adult plumage. The young are more puzzling. There is always some white in the underwing coverts, whereas in the Golden, they are always dark (see p. 35).

White-tailed Kite   ws 39"

Slender, small, long-tailed and white with dark wingtips and round black carpal patches. In active flight, more often seen gliding than soaring. Hovers on rapidly beating wings.

juv.

♀

♂

Northern Harrier   ws 43"

Glides and flies low, buoyantly twisting and turning over open grassy ground. From above shows a white rump in all plumages. During courtship and autumn migration, soars higher in the sky.

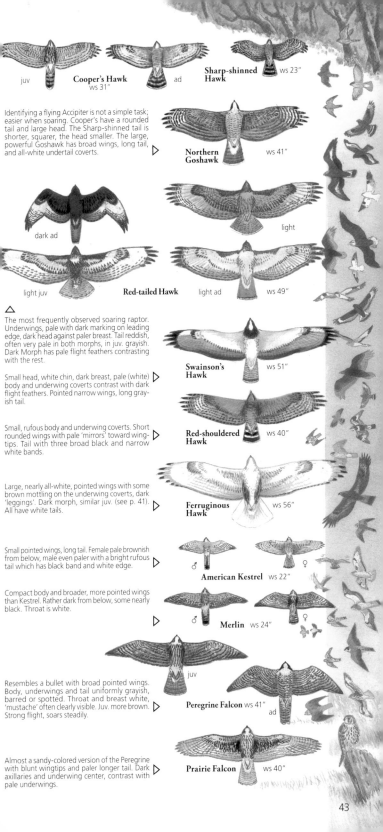

juv

Cooper's Hawk
ws 31"

ad

Sharp-shinned Hawk ws 23"

Identifying a flying Accipiter is not a simple task; easier when soaring. Cooper's have a rounded tail and large head. The Sharp-shinned tail is shorter, squarer, the head smaller. The large, powerful Goshawk has broad wings, long tail, and all-white undertail coverts. ▷

Northern Goshawk ws 41"

dark ad

light

light juv

Red-tailed Hawk light ad ws 49"

△
The most frequently observed soaring raptor. Underwings, pale with dark marking on leading edge, dark head against paler breast. Tail reddish, often very pale in both morphs, in juv. grayish. Dark Morph has pale flight feathers contrasting with the rest.

Small head, white chin, dark breast, pale (white) body and underwing coverts contrast with dark flight feathers. Pointed narrow wings, long grayish tail. ▷

Swainson's Hawk ws 51"

Small, rufous body and underwing coverts. Short rounded wings with pale 'mirrors' toward wing-tips. Tail with three broad black and narrow white bands. ▷

Red-shouldered Hawk ws 40"

Large, nearly all-white, pointed wings with some brown mottling on the underwing coverts, dark 'leggings'. Dark morph, similar juv. (see p. 41). All have white tails. ▷

Ferruginous Hawk ws 56"

Small pointed wings, long tail. Female pale brownish from below, male even paler with a bright rufous tail which has black band and white edge. ▷

♂   ♀

American Kestrel ws 22"

Compact body and broader, more pointed wings than Kestrel. Rather dark from below, some nearly black. Throat is white. ▷

♂   ♀

Merlin ws 24"

Resembles a bullet with broad pointed wings. Body, underwings and tail uniformly grayish, barred or spotted. Throat and breast white, 'mustache' often clearly visible. Juv. more brown. Strong flight, soars steadily. ▷

juv

Peregrine Falcon ws 41"

ad

Almost a sandy-colored version of the Peregrine with blunt wingtips and paler longer tail. Dark axillaries and underwing center, contrast with pale underwings. ▷

Prairie Falcon ws 40"

43

Kestrel

Kite p. 36

● **Falcons** *Falconidae* 4 sp. Diurnal raptors with long pointed wings. Do not build their own nest. Like owls, but unlike hawks, they kill their prey by biting into the neck while holding it with only one claw. When curious, the young birds hiss like owls and bob their heads.

◁ **Kestrels**, as all birds of prey, have remarkable eyesight. From a high lookout perch or when soaring over open grassland, they can spot a grasshopper in vegetation, fly toward their prey, stall in the air and hover before swooping down to catch their meal. Kestrels are well known for this but are not the only raptor to hunt this way. Rough-legged Hawks also hover, sometimes with wings flapping, and the Osprey usually hovers before plunging down into water to catch a fish.

In common with the Pygmy Owl, the Kestrel has a pair of false eyes on the back of its head. These two dark spots, more pronounced in the male, is a defense against predators who might think the bird is watching them.

American Kestrel cW, fS
Falco sparverius

L 9" **Habitat**: Pastures, grassy fields, open woodland, oak savannah, edges of towns, lake shores, etc. Nests in old woodpecker holes, accepts nest boxes.

Kestrels are real opportunists and will occupy any open habitat where they can find food. The absence of cavities for nesting limits their distribution. Kestrels benefit from the nest box program for Wood Ducks. Formerly called Sparrow Hawks, they eat almost exclusively large insects like grasshoppers, crickets, etc., as well as spiders and small rodents. Birds in suburban Settings often change their prey and specialize on House Sparrows, when the old name fits.

Merlin rW
Falco columbarius

L. 10" An uncommon migrant and winter visitor from the prairies and open northern forests. Most likely found in association with flocks of shorebirds in the tidal district, or with finches and sparrow flocks wherever they occur, usually in open woodland and edge habitats. Feeds almost entirely on birds up to its own size but may attack larger ones. Occasionally takes small rodents and dragonflies. Not much larger than a Kestrel, shorter tail, more compact, like a miniature Peregrine Falcon. Hunts with a dashing, very fast and direct flight often low over ground; may hover.

◁ The **Pacific Black Merlin** breeds along the coastal region from Alaska to British Columbia. Mostly sedentary but some move southwards in winter and could occur in Napa. It would be difficult to identify them in flight but Merlins like to perch on the ground, often for a long time and with little fear of man. Then easy to observe and identify.

♀ wings and back nearly black

Peregrine Falcon   xW, lrP
Falco peregrinus

L 16" **Habitat**: Open areas, nests in cavities in cliff faces such as the Palisades above Calistoga. Hunts and breeds around Lake Berryessa. In winter seen in the marshes.

Before 1970 this beautiful falcon was nearly extinct in California. Fewer than ten pairs nested, one of them in Napa. Following the ban on DDT in 1972 and with recovery, several pairs now breed in the county. They can be observed in very unusual places. I saw one flying over the city of Napa and sketched another perched on boulders in the salt evaporators. A very dark bird with an almost completely black 'helmet' and some white on the cheeks. A bird at the northern end of Lake Berryessa had a more pronounced 'mustache' clearly visible in flight, with a pinkish breast.

Prairie Falcon   lrP
Falco mexicanus

L 16" **Habitat**: Dry grassy country and open woodland at Blue Ridge where they breed. Nest in a cavity near the top of a cliff. In winter occasionally seen in the marshes.

More agile than the Peregrine but has a different hunting technique. Flies rapidly, only 10-20 feet above ground, and preys mostly on ground squirrels and meadowlarks. With slightly longer tail and more rounded wings than the Peregrine, is well adapted to catch prey on the ground, while the Peregrine, with pointed wings, is an aerial hunter of small and medium-sized birds. Most likely seen hunting on the northern shore of Lake Berryessa. I watched two harassing a soaring Golden Eagle that finally gave up and flew away.

45

California females lay up to 25 eggs in one clutch. The large brood is reared by both parents and the chick can flutter when only 10 days old, to escape.

♂,♀ duller

● **Pheasants** *Phasianidae* 2 introduced sp. Pheasants are an Old World family of over 150 species. Since pheasants and the very different turkey can produce hybrids by artificial insemination, all are now included in one family.

▽

● **American Quail** *Odontophoridae*, 2 sp. Many years ago New World quail (32 species) were included with Old World partridge, pheasant and grouse in one large family. Research shows they separated in the distant past and are not closely related.

California Quail
Callipepla californica
cP

L 10" **Habitat**: Found all over the county, except in the marshes. Prefers chaparral and open woodland with dense cover. Seen along roadsides and in rural backyards.

Usually seen in pairs or coveys feeding on the ground. Always active but not shy. Runs very fast in a slender, upright posture before disappearing into dense cover. When relaxed, is bold and appears round. The male's loud call 'chi-CHA-go' is a typical country sound. Coveys keep in contact by clucking and spitting notes. Autumn hunting does not seem to reduce their population. They roost in low trees or bushes, to be less vulnerable to night predators.

Mountain Quail
Oreortyx pictus
fP

L 11" **Habitat**: Hills with rocky slopes and plenty of dense cover from 300 feet to close to the top of Mount St. Helena. Access to freshwater is very important.

During my fieldwork I heard their loud resonant call, 'KYork,' many times from the slopes across the valley but although just a few yards away, I didn't get a glimpse of the bird. Driving up to Mount St. Helena, a bird that flew over the road might have been this fairly common but so secretive quail. The female usually lays 7-10 eggs in a clutch and both parents take care of the brood.

crown

♂

♀

Ring-necked Pheasant
Phasianus colchicus
uP, introd

L ♂ 35", ♀ 21" **Habitat**: Locally introduced. Thrives best on multi-crop agricultural land and on the edges of tidal marshes which resemble their original habitat. Female makes her nest in dense herbaceous cover. Needs low trees in which to roost at night.

Pheasants, of Chinese origins, introduced on several occasions. Now there is a small self-sustaining population. The loud, harsh crow of the cock ,'Kor-Kok,' can be heard at a considerable distance followed by a short burst of whirring wingbeats. When feeling alone, young birds make a curious double piping sound followed by a creaking third note.

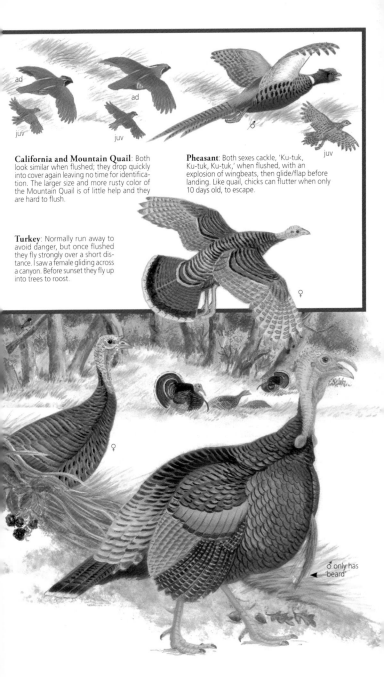

California and Mountain Quail: Both look similar when flushed; they drop quickly into cover again leaving no time for identification. The larger size and more rusty color of the Mountain Quail is of little help and they are hard to flush.

Pheasant: Both sexes cackle, 'Ku-tuk, Ku-tuk, Ku-tuk,' when flushed, with an explosion of wingbeats, then glide/flap before landing. Like quail, chicks can flutter when only 10 days old, to escape.

Turkey: Normally run away to avoid danger, but once flushed they fly strongly over a short distance. I saw a female gliding across a canyon. Before sunset they fly up into trees to roost.

♀ only has 'beard'

Not native to Napa County. First attempts to establish them around 1920 failed but releases since 1970, with wild birds from Texas, were successful and turkeys are now seen and heard throughout the county, even walking across lawn. Normally very wary, but when unmolested can become confident, and flocks of 5 to 30 and more can be observed. A gobbler weighs between 16 and 17 lbs. and a hen 9 lbs.

Wild Turkey
Meleagris gallopavo

fP, introd.

L ♂46", ♀27" **Habitat**: Wooded agricultural areas, open oak forest, dry slopes and open chaparral. Visit rural backyards. Nest on ground under shrubby cover or against a fallen log.

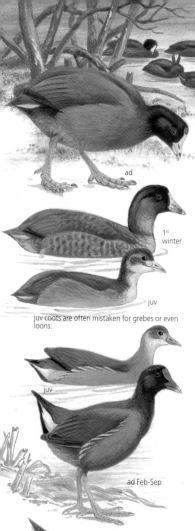

Moorhen

Coots have a small (**moorhens** a large) white mark on the side of the tail and swim with jerky forward movements.

● **Rails** *Rallidae* 6 sp. Marsh birds with short tails, rounded wings and dangling legs in flight. Many species are shy and secretive, hiding in dense vegetation. The Coot and Moorhen are more aquatic and easier to observe.

American Coot cW, rS
Fulica americana

L 15" **Habitat**: Freshwater ponds, lakes and reservoirs. In winter also open sheltered, brackish waters. Likes to graze on lawns nearby. Nest: a bulky cup built over water in waterside vegetation.

Resembles a dumpy dark duck, bobbing its head when swimming. Patters across water before taking flight. On land looks like a clumsy chicken with thick white bill, long legs, big feet with lobes along toes. An uncommon breeding bird but well distributed over the entire county. In winter this changes. Hundreds arrive from the north and concentrate on large, tight rafts in open waters. Often seen grazing on golf courses or park lawns, where they can be very tame.

Common Moorhen lrP
Gallinula chloropus

L 14" **Habitat**: Small, freshwater ponds in marshes with dense vegetation and low-growing willows. Nest is usually well hidden, over water.

Not shy but more retiring than the coot and also more solitary, or lives in pairs. Never far from cover. When swimming away from the observer, the white 'flags' under the tail show up very well. White stripe on the flanks and the red shield and bill are both good field marks. As with other rails, they have long, un-lobed toes.

Sora elrP
Porzana carolina

L 9" **Habitat**: Need shallow freshwater with extensive vegetative cover, such as sedges and cattail, for breeding. In winter, also in tidal marshes, with mudbanks.

The most likely rail to be observed but is generally hidden in dense vegetation and only heard. The Sora will come out of cover to walk along edges of vegetation in search of small insects, worms, molluscs and any other small animal. They flush more readily than the other rails and drop quickly into cover again. It is not known if they still nest in the county. The only breeding record is from Conn Creek in 1975.

Voice: The spring call is a clear, quail-like whistle that rises at the end, 'Ker-wee,' repeated over and over again, day and night with monotonous regularity. Most characteristic is a high, squealing whinny, 'ca-WEEee-e-e-e-e-ee-eep,' slowing and ascending at the end. When alarmed, a surprisingly loud and sharp 'Keek' is heard out of the cover.

juv coots are often mistaken for grebes or even loons.

Rails can be noisy birds. Coots and moorhens make different clucking and whining notes. Large wintering rafts of coots often make a curious roaring sound on water when a predator appears or when running together, splashing over the water to take flight–a sound that can be heard a long way off. The calls of all rails are important in communicating their presence.

48

The precocial downy chick of the larger rails could be mistaken for a Black Rail, except for its shape. They are quite agile.

Clapper Rail chick

All rails can swim, and Clapper Rails are sometimes seen crossing a channel; they do not dive for food as do coots.

juv

ad

imm

ad

Black Rail

IrP

Laterallus jamaicensis

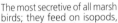
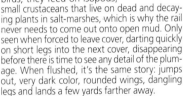

L 6" **Habitat:** Inaccessible tidal salt-marshes with dense cover, where they build their nest in tuft grass or *Salicornia*.

The most secretive of all marsh birds; they feed on isopods, small crustaceans that live on dead and decaying plants in salt-marshes, which is why the rail never needs to come out onto open mud. Only seen when forced to leave cover, darting quickly on short legs into the next cover, disappearing before there is time to see any detail of the plumage. When flushed, it's the same story: jumps out, very dark color, rounded wings, dangling legs and lands a few yards farther away.

Voice: This little rail has been recorded in the county, mainly by voice alone. Seldom heard in daytime, most active in the middle of the night, when there's no-one about, especially in bright moonlight and low temperatures. The male calls with a nasal 'Kic-Kic-Keerr,' sometimes growling, 'grr-grr-grr,' and the female calls 'croo-croo-croo.' A sparrow-like note, 'KiK' or 'twirr,' can also be heard.

Clapper Rail

IrP

Rallus longirostris

L 15" **Habitat:** Tidal wetland, in salt and brackish water with dense cover of pickleweed and cord grass. Nest chiefly inside a grass tuft or clump of rushes.

Large, long-billed and usually impossible to see, that's a Clapper Rail. One can sometimes see their chicken-like tracks on open mudflats close to cover. Their main food is crabs, snails, mussels and worms. When flushed out of cover, the pale wings and long, pale dangling legs are typical. (Virginia Rails have darker wings and red legs.) Sedentary, with a patchy distribution around San Francisco Bay. Only a limited number breed in Napa marshes. Mostly solitary.

Voice: Calls in the evening, early morning and also at night. Territorial call is a loud, rapidly repeated 'chack, chack.' The monotonous attraction call is a series of hard 'Ket' and some fast, unmusical 'Keck' calls. Often so noisy that it's possible to mistake a single pair for several birds, and it's also difficult to locate the direction from which the birds call.

Virginia Rail

IuP

Rallus limicola

L 9½" **Habitat:** Marshes and sloughs with reeds, cattails and other dense cover. Nest is built over water in tussock-grass or other vegetation.

The most common rail in the county. We heard a rail calling from marshy ponds surrounded by new vineyards where there was a colony of 300 pairs of courting Tricolored Blackbirds. As a rail called from dense cover a few yards from my feet, a small-black bird flushed. I thought it was a Black Rail. This would have been unusual in freshwater; however, it was a juvenile, nearly all-black Virginia Rail.

Voice: Pairs keep contact with a duet of pig-like grunts–'oink, oink' notes. The courtship call is a metallic 'Kik Kid Kidick Kidick' and sometimes a harsh 'werk-werk-werk-werk.' In spring, a series of loud, rapid 'Ki Ki' notes followed by 'Krrr' is often heard. This seems to be the call of a female attracting a partner.

American   Pacific

Pluvialis In early spring they molt into their br. plumage. In a flock you will see birds with differently advanced black belly patterns. To find a 'Golden' between them, look for their outlines.

● **Plovers** *Charadriidae* 5 sp. Short-billed, large rounded heads. When feeding, run for a short distance and stop. Head often nervously bobbing. Gregarious out of breeding season but never seen in such large flocks as sandpipers. (For birds in flight, see p. 56.)

Black-bellied Plover
Pluvialis squatarola
fW

L 11½" Large, big-headed, with a stout bill and, in winter rather pale plumage. In br. plumage, face and underparts are strikingly black. Mostly seen on open mudflats, rarely on grassy fields or pasture; usually singles, or in a small flock, but sometimes abundant beside the 'wader crowd,' when they often stand motionless for a long time, with all heads windward. Their triple flight call is a melancholy 'tee-oo-ee,' with lower middle note.

Pacific Golden Plover
Pluvialis fulva
lxT

L 10¼" Pacific and American Golden Plovers are so similar that only an expert can tell them apart in the field. The Pacific is slightly more elegant with longer legs and bill. In winter plumage it is more golden and in br. plumage has mottled flanks and undertail coverts; but beware of molting Americans. The common call is 'ch-**ee**' and in flight a whistling, 'chu-it.'

American Golden Plover
Pluvialis dominica
lxT

L 10½" Both Goldens like dry mudflats and short grassy fields. Will visit golf courses. Not yet recorded but could occur one day. The American has longer wingtips and shorter legs, and in winter is grayer. In br. plumage (see above), flanks and undertail coverts are jet black. Most easily distinguished by their calls; in flight an urgent '**clu**-ee,' unlike the Pacific's, and the display call, sometimes heard before leaving for their northern breeding haunts, is a trisyllabic '**dlu**-ee-uh.'

Snowy Plover
Charadrius alexandrinus
lrS

L 6¼" **Habitat**: In winter, dry mudflats; normally breed on coastal beach. Napa birds have adapted to salt evaporation ponds where a few now breed and stay all year round.

They resemble little toys when running away on their long legs. The head, in relation to their rather short body, is big. The female is drab in color, in between the male and nbr. plumages. The California population is very small and every effort should be made to preserve Napa's few breeding Snowys. Seldom seen in small flocks, mostly solitary or in pairs, though small flocks may roost together in winter.

Semipalmated Plover
Charadrius semipalmatus
luW

L 7¼" A winter visitor on the mudflats, sometimes seen in large flocks. Singles can visit the broad Lake Berryessa shores. Much darker in color than the resident Snowy. Most striking are the darker cheeks, longer body with more pointed rear end and especially the bright yellow legs and bicolored bill. Their flight call is a short whistle 'tu-**wee**' while the Snowy's is a rapid 'Kwip.'

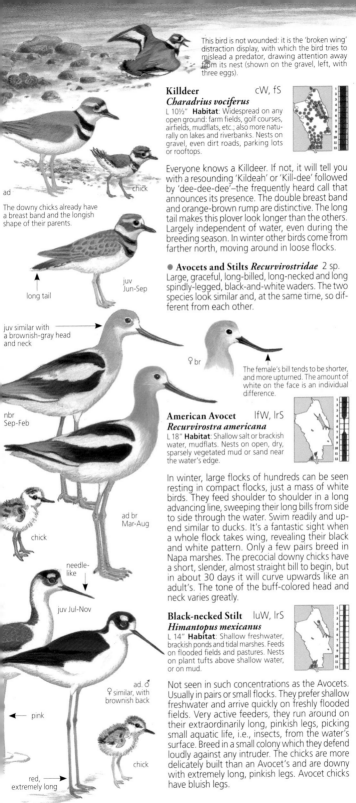

This bird is not wounded: it is the 'broken wing' distraction display, with which the bird tries to mislead a predator, drawing attention away from its nest (shown on the gravel, left, with three eggs).

Killdeer
cW, fS
Charadrius vociferus
L 10½" **Habitat:** Widespread on any open ground: farm fields, golf courses, airfields, mudflats, etc.; also more naturally on lakes and riverbanks. Nests on gravel, even dirt roads, parking lots or rooftops.

Everyone knows a Killdeer. If not, it will tell you with a resounding 'Kildeah' or 'Kill-dee' followed by 'dee-dee-dee'–the frequently heard call that announces its presence. The double breast band and orange-brown rump are distinctive. The long tail makes this plover look longer than the others. Largely independent of water, even during the breeding season. In winter other birds come from farther north, moving around in loose flocks.

ad

chick

The downy chicks already have a breast band and the longish shape of their parents.

juv Jun-Sep

long tail

● **Avocets and Stilts** *Recurvirostridae* 2 sp.
Large, graceful, long-billed, long-necked and long spindly-legged, black-and-white waders. The two species look similar and, at the same time, so different from each other.

juv similar with a brownish-gray head and neck

♀ br

The female's bill tends to be shorter, and more upturned. The amount of white on the face is an individual difference.

nbr Sep-Feb

American Avocet
IfW, lrS
Recurvirostra americana
L 18" **Habitat:** Shallow salt or brackish water, mudflats. Nests on open, dry, sparsely vegetated mud or sand near the water's edge.

ad br Mar-Aug

chick

In winter, large flocks of hundreds can be seen resting in compact flocks, just a mass of white birds. They feed shoulder to shoulder in a long advancing line, sweeping their long bills from side to side through the water. Swim readily and up-end similar to ducks. It's a fantastic sight when a whole flock takes wing, revealing their black and white pattern. Only a few pairs breed in Napa marshes. The precocial downy chicks have a short, slender, almost straight bill to begin, but in about 30 days it will curve upwards like an adult's. The tone of the buff-colored head and neck varies greatly.

needle-like

juv Jul-Nov

Black-necked Stilt
luW, lrS
Himantopus mexicanus
L 14" **Habitat:** Shallow freshwater, brackish ponds and tidal marshes. Feeds on flooded fields and pastures. Nests on plant tufts above shallow water, or on mud.

ad. ♂ ♀ similar, with brownish back

pink

chick

red, extremely long

Not seen in such concentrations as the Avocets. Usually in pairs or small flocks. They prefer shallow freshwater and arrive quickly on freshly flooded fields. Very active feeders, they run around on their extraordinarily long, pinkish legs, picking small aquatic life, i.e., insects, from the water's surface. Breed in a small colony which they defend loudly against any intruder. The chicks are more delicately built than an Avocet's and are downy with extremely long, pinkish legs. Avocet chicks have bluish legs.

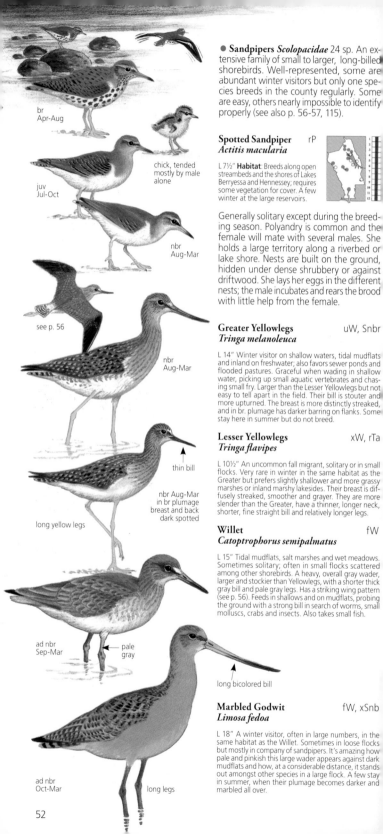

br
Apr-Aug

chick, tended
mostly by male
alone

juv
Jul-Oct

nbr
Aug-Mar

see p. 56

nbr
Aug-Mar

thin bill

nbr Aug-Mar
in br plumage
breast and back
dark spotted

long yellow legs

ad nbr
Sep-Mar

pale
gray

long bicolored bill

ad nbr
Oct-Mar

long legs

● **Sandpipers** *Scolopacidae* 24 sp. An extensive family of small to larger, long-billed shorebirds. Well-represented, some are abundant winter visitors but only one species breeds in the county regularly. Some are easy, others nearly impossible to identify properly (see also p. 56-57, 115).

Spotted Sandpiper rP
Actitis macularia

L 7½" **Habitat**: Breeds along open streambeds and the shores of Lakes Berryessa and Hennessey; requires some vegetation for cover. A few winter at the large reservoirs.

Generally solitary except during the breeding season. Polyandry is common and the female will mate with several males. She holds a large territory along a riverbed or lake shore. Nests are built on the ground, hidden under dense shrubbery or against driftwood. She lays her eggs in the different nests; the male incubates and rears the brood with little help from the female.

Greater Yellowlegs uW, Snbr
Tringa melanoleuca

L 14" Winter visitor on shallow waters, tidal mudflats and inland on freshwater; also favors sewer ponds and flooded pastures. Graceful when wading in shallow water, picking up small aquatic vertebrates and chasing small fry. Larger than the Lesser Yellowlegs but not easy to tell apart in the field. Their bill is stouter and more upturned. The breast is more distinctly streaked, and in br. plumage has darker barring on flanks. Some stay here in summer but do not breed.

Lesser Yellowlegs xW, rTa
Tringa flavipes

L 10½" An uncommon fall migrant, solitary or in small flocks. Very rare in winter in the same habitat as the Greater but prefers slightly shallower and more grassy marshes or inland marshy lakesides. Their breast is diffusely streaked, smoother and grayer. They are more slender than the Greater, have a thinner, longer neck, shorter, fine straight bill and relatively longer legs.

Willet fW
Catoptrophorus semipalmatus

L 15" Tidal mudflats, salt marshes and wet meadows. Sometimes solitary; often in small flocks scattered among other shorebirds. A heavy, overall gray wader, larger and stockier than Yellowlegs, with a shorter thick gray bill and pale gray legs. Has a striking wing pattern (see p. 56). Feeds in shallows and on mudflats, probing the ground with a strong bill in search of worms, small molluscs, crabs and insects. Also takes small fish.

Marbled Godwit fW, xSnb
Limosa fedoa

L 18" A winter visitor, often in large numbers, in the same habitat as the Willet. Sometimes in loose flocks but mostly in company of sandpipers. It's amazing how pale and pinkish this large wader appears against dark mudflats and how, at a considerable distance, it stands out amongst other species in a large flock. A few stay in summer, when their plumage becomes darker and marbled all over.

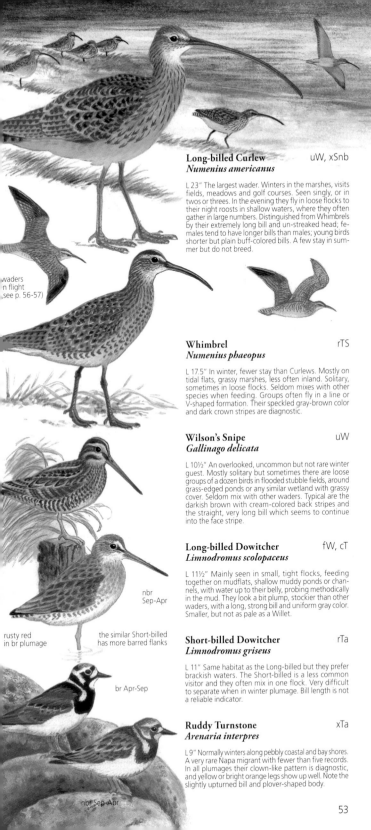

waders
in flight
(see p. 56-57)

Long-billed Curlew uW, xSnb
Numenius americanus

L 23" The largest wader. Winters in the marshes, visits fields, meadows and golf courses. Seen singly, or in twos or threes. In the evening they fly in loose flocks to their night roosts in shallow waters, where they often gather in large numbers. Distinguished from Whimbrels by their extremely long bill and un-streaked head; females tend to have longer bills than males; young birds shorter but plain buff-colored bills. A few stay in summer but do not breed.

Whimbrel rTS
Numenius phaeopus

L 17.5" In winter, fewer stay than Curlews. Mostly on tidal flats, grassy marshes, less often inland. Solitary, sometimes in loose flocks. Seldom mixes with other species when feeding. Groups often fly in a line or V-shaped formation. Their speckled gray-brown color and dark crown stripes are diagnostic.

Wilson's Snipe uW
Gallinago delicata

L 10½" An overlooked, uncommon but not rare winter guest. Mostly solitary but sometimes there are loose groups of a dozen birds in flooded stubble fields, around grass-edged ponds or any similar wetland with grassy cover. Seldom mix with other waders. Typical are the darkish brown with cream-colored back stripes and the straight, very long bill which seems to continue into the face stripe.

Long-billed Dowitcher fW, cT
Limnodromus scolopaceus

L 11½" Mainly seen in small, tight flocks, feeding together on mudflats, shallow muddy ponds or channels, with water up to their belly, probing methodically in the mud. They look a bit plump, stockier than other waders, with a long, strong bill and uniform gray color. Smaller, but not as pale as a Willet.

nbr
Sep-Apr

rusty red
in br plumage

the similar Short-billed
has more barred flanks

Short-billed Dowitcher rTa
Limnodromus griseus

L 11" Same habitat as the Long-billed but they prefer brackish waters. The Short-billed is a less common visitor and they often mix in one flock. Very difficult to separate when in winter plumage. Bill length is not a reliable indicator.

br Apr-Sep

Ruddy Turnstone xTa
Arenaria interpres

L 9" Normally winters along pebbly coastal and bay shores. A very rare Napa migrant with fewer than five records. In all plumages their clown-like pattern is diagnostic, and yellow or bright orange legs show up well. Note the slightly upturned bill and plover-shaped body.

nbr Sep-Apr

53

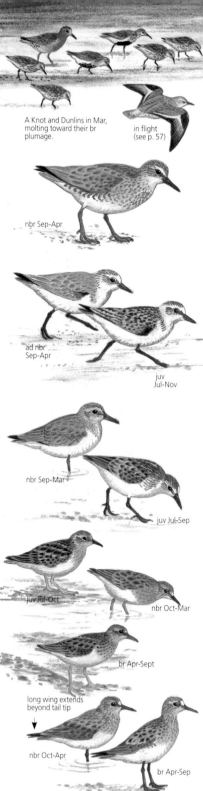

A Knot and Dunlins in Mar, molting toward their br plumage.

in flight (see p. 57)

nbr Sep-Apr

ad nbr Sep-Apr

juv Jul-Nov

nbr Sep-Mar

juv Jul-Sep

juv Jul-Oct

nbr Oct-Mar

br Apr-Sept

long wing extends beyond tail tip

nbr Oct-Apr

br Apr-Sep

● 'Peeps': The Least, Semipalmated and Western Sandpipers are generally referred to as peeps, after their flight calls.

For many beginners, sandpipers are the most difficult birds (besides sparrows) to identify. At first they all look alike and also have many different plumages: winter, summer and juvenile as well as transitional stages as they molt from one plumage to the next. All have similar habits and often stay together in large flocks on open mudflats.

Red Knot   xW, xTS, nb
Calidris canutus

L 10½" The easiest sandpiper to recognize, but only by size. Nearly as large as the Black-bellied Plover with which they often associate in flocks together with the smaller turnstones. All have a similar way of feeding, pecking their food from the mud's surface. Rather short-legged, plump and much larger than a similarly colored Dunlin. Rather thick bill, almost straight, medium length. They like sandy beaches and therefore never form large flocks on local mudflats.

Sanderling   xW
Calidris alba

L 8" Not too difficult to recognize in any plumage. Strikingly paler in winter than any other little wader, with a blackish patch on shoulder although this is often invisible when covered by breast feathers. In spring (Apr.May) can resemble one of the smaller molting peeps but the stronger bill and behavior are distinctive. They run up and down beaches with the waves, even more than the Red Knot, a bird of sandy beaches. In Napa County there are three records of a total of four birds.

Western Sandpiper   fW, cTS, fTa
Calidris mauri

L 6½" A winter visitor in Napa County. The Western and Semipalmated (see p. 115) are very similar in appearance but the Western has a longer, slightly drooping bill and paler face. Westerns have a whiter breast. The smaller Semipalmated's bill is shorter and straight; it is a bit darker and has a well-marked breastband, while the Western has a whiter breast. The differences are very small and it's not easy to separate them. The Western occurs in very large flocks on the tidal mudflats.

Least Sandpiper   fW, cTS, fTa
Calidris minutilla

L 6" The smallest of all the peeps. Smaller than a House Sparrow which weighs almost 1 oz., this wader's weight is only 0.7 oz. Slightly darker and browner than the other peeps, with a darker breast and a very thin, slightly drooping bill. Since all others have black legs, their greenish-yellow legs are diagnostic. Their frequent crouching posture is typical. Never found in such large flocks as the Westerns. Most birds are observed during migration from the end of Jul., with a peak at the end of Sep. Winters on mudflats and inland at grassy wetlands.

Baird's Sandpiper   lxTa
Calidris bairdii

L 7½" Delicate build, long-bodied, short-legged, with a rather pale buff head and breast. Beware confusion with the Sanderling, which has a similar transitional plumage but longer legs and a stouter bill. Least Sandpipers are smaller, with thinner bills. A fall migrant, staying in Napa from mid-Jul. to the end of Oct. Mixes with other peeps in their large flocks but when feeding stays apart in small groups of 2-5 birds at the dry edges of mudflats, or even further inland on dry, short grass fields. They wade in water or forage over mud less frequently than other sandpipers. They winter in South America as far south as Chile.

Dunlin
Calidris alpina
fW, cTS, rTa

L 8½" With the Western, this is one of the two most abundant visitors on Napa's mudflats. Easy to identify and the best bird to study for changes in plumage. From mid-Sep. flocks of birds arrive in nbr. dress. Most winter residents are on the mudflats until Apr., by which time they have changed into br. plumage with typical black belly. From mid-May until mid-Aug. they are in their breeding haunts in the far north.

juv
Jul-Sep

br
Apr-Aug

nbr
Aug-Mar

Pectoral Sandpiper
Calidris melanotos
lrTa

L 8¾" A passage migrant. Can be seen on tidal flats and also on grassy-edged freshwaters from mid-Aug. to early Nov. An abundant spring migrant in central North America. They remind me of an overgrown Least Sandpiper or even more of a small Ruff (p. 115), which I know so well in Europe. Larger than a Dunlin, they have a more erect stance and a longish neck. There's a clear divide between streaked breast and white belly. Yellowish legs like the Least Sandpiper.

br
Apr-Oct

The ♂ is much larger than the ♀ and nbr. birds are grayer.

nbr Nov-Mar

● **Phalarope:** A monstrous name for such elegant birds, a combination of ancient Greek, *phalaris* = coot and *pous* = foot (Coot-footed wader). There are only three species worldwide, and all visit Napa. Small, rather tame waders that swim buoyantly, like small gulls, often spinning round in circles, picking insects off the water's surface.

All phalarope males are dull in color; they incubate and rear the brood while the female pairs with another male.

♀ br Apr-Jul

needle-like bill

Wilson's Phalarope
Phalaropus tricolor
xW, ex, lrTa

L 9¼" A common fall but rare spring migrant. Most birds are seen on shallow ponds or grassy marshes from mid-Jul. till the end of Sep. Mostly solitary or in small groups. Wader-like in its habits. Swims less than other phalaropes; readily walks in shallow water, pecking insects from the water's surface. The nbr. ad. resembles a Lesser Yellowlegs (p. 52) but is much paler, has a needle-like bill and the yellow legs are shorter. Some stay during summer and may possibly breed as the marshes are restored.

♀ br Apr-Jul

♀ nbr Aug-Mar
some can look very pale, nearly white

♀ br Apr-Sep

Red Phalarope
Phalaropus fulicarius
xTa

L 8½" An Arctic tundra breeder, pelagic during migration and in winter. Heavy storms often drive large numbers toward the coast and some farther inland. Same size as a Dunlin and often very tame. Usually seen swimming. A very pale, plain gray bird, with white head and breast, and a black mark on hindcrown and cheeks. The bill is rather thick. The br. plumage is unmistakable but unlikely to be seen in Napa.

nbr
Aug-Mar

Red-necked Phalarope
Phalaropus lobatus
rTs

L 7¾" Also breeds on tundra ponds. During winter leads a pelagic life far from land, mostly in small flocks. A common migrant, often in flocks of 100 or more at salt evaporation ponds. The smallest of the three phalaropes, with a needle-like bill. The gray back has paler streaks. The cheeks are dark, like a mask, and the hindcrown has a black cap. The juveniles of all three species resemble their parents in shape but have more *Calidris*-like brownish, paler striped backs and head patterns.

♀ br Apr-Jul

nbr Aug-Apr

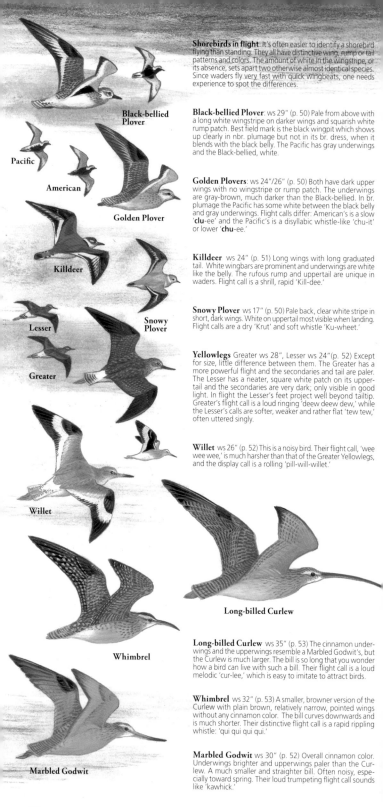

Shorebirds in flight: It's often easier to identify a shorebird flying than standing. They all have distinctive wing, rump or tail patterns and colors. The amount of white in the wingstripe, or its absence, sets apart two otherwise almost identical species. Since waders fly very fast with quick wingbeats, one needs experience to spot the differences.

Black-bellied Plover: ws 29" (p. 50) Pale from above with a long white wingstripe on darker wings and squarish white rump patch. Best field mark is the black wingpit which shows up clearly in nbr. plumage but not in its br. dress, when it blends with the black belly. The Pacific has gray underwings and the Black-bellied, white.

Golden Plovers: ws 24"/26" (p. 50) Both have dark upper wings with no wingstripe or rump patch. The underwings are gray-brown, much darker than the Black-bellied. In br. plumage the Pacific has some white between the black belly and gray underwings. Flight calls differ: American's is a slow 'clu-ee' and the Pacific's is a disyllabic whistle-like 'chu-it' or lower 'chu-ee.'

Killdeer ws 24" (p. 51) Long wings with long graduated tail. White wingbars are prominent and underwings are white like the belly. The rufous rump and uppertail are unique in waders. Flight call is a shrill, rapid 'Kill-dee.'

Snowy Plover ws 17" (p. 50) Pale back, clear white stripe in short, dark wings. White on uppertail most visible when landing. Flight calls are a dry 'Krut' and soft whistle 'Ku-wheet.'

Yellowlegs Greater ws 28", Lesser ws 24"(p. 52) Except for size, little difference between them. The Greater has a more powerful flight and the secondaries and tail are paler. The Lesser has a neater, square white patch on its upper-tail and the secondaries are very dark; only visible in good light. In flight the Lesser's feet project well beyond tailtip. Greater's flight call is a loud ringing 'deew deew dew,' while the Lesser's calls are softer, weaker and rather flat 'tew tew,' often uttered singly.

Willet ws 26" (p. 52) This is a noisy bird. Their flight call, 'wee wee wee,' is much harsher than that of the Greater Yellowlegs, and the display call is a rolling 'pill-will-willet.'

Long-billed Curlew ws 35" (p. 53) The cinnamon under-wings and the upperwings resemble a Marbled Godwit's, but the Curlew is much larger. The bill is so long that you wonder how a bird can live with such a bill. Their flight call is a loud melodic 'cur-lee,' which is easy to imitate to attract birds.

Whimbrel ws 32" (p. 53) A smaller, browner version of the Curlew with plain brown, relatively narrow, pointed wings without any cinnamon color. The bill curves downwards and is much shorter. Their distinctive flight call is a rapid rippling whistle: 'qui qui qui qui.'

Marbled Godwit ws 30" (p. 52) Overall cinnamon color. Underwings brighter and upperwings paler than the Cur-lew. A much smaller and straighter bill. Often noisy, espe-cially toward spring. Their loud trumpeting flight call sounds like 'kawhick.'

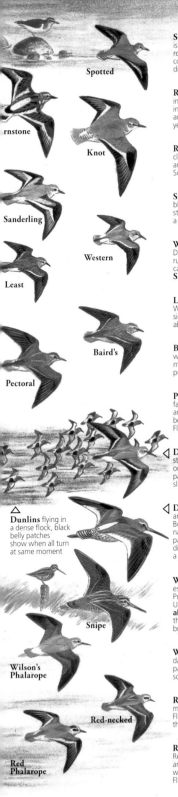

Spotted Sandpiper ws 15" (p. 52) The most typical flight is low over water with stiff rapid shallow wingbeats on short rounded wings. The striking black and white underwing coverts are only seen when high in the air during courtship display. Flight call is a clear whistle 'tweet wee.'

Ruddy Turnstone ws 21" (p. 53) From above, a strikingly bold dark and white pattern on wings, rump and tail, in all plumages. From below, very white with dark breast and head. Flight calls: a chuckling 'tuk-a-tuk-tuk' or short yelping 'k-l-ew.'

Red Knot ws 23" (p. 54) Plain gray from above, with narrow clear-cut but faint wingstripe and pale gray rump. Underwings are also gray; belly paler. Rather silent, especially single birds. Sometimes a low husky 'knutt' can be heard.

Sanderling ws 17" (p. 54) Pale, nearly white with a broad black leading edge to the forewing and a broad white wingstripe. Underside is almost entirely snow white. Flight call is a hard repetitive 'kwip.'

Western Sandpiper ws 14" (p. 54) Smaller and paler than Dunlin with a faint narrow wingbar and white sides to the rump and uppertail. Sides of tail gray, center dark. Flight call: a thin, sharp, high-pitched 'cheet.' The **Semipalmated Sandpiper** (p. 115) is very similar but a bit darker.

Least Sandpiper ws 13" (p. 54) Smaller and darker than Western, with a narrow white stripe on shorter wings. White side to rump and uppertail. Tail has gray edges. Flight call variable, a musical rising trill 'preep' or 'trreeet.'

Baird's Sandpiper ws 17" (p. 54) In flight appears long-winged with inconspicuous wingstripe. Rump and uppertail mostly brown, edged with a little white. Flight call: a short purring trill, 'prrreet.'

Pectoral Sandpiper ws 18" (p. 55) Dark wings with a very faint narrow wingstripe. Broad blackish center on white rump and gray edges to a slightly pointed tail. A sharp difference between the dark breast and white belly is visible from below. Flight call is a loud, harsh, short 'churk' or 'trrit.'

◁ **Dunlin** ws 17" (p. 55) Plain gray with a clear white wingstripe, broader than other sandpipers. A narrow, dark center on white rump. Underwings and belly white; has a large black patch on white belly in br. plumage. Flight call is a distinctive slurred 'kreee' or 'treep.'

△

Dunlins flying in a dense flock, black belly patches show when all turn at same moment

◁ **Dowitchers** ws 19" (p. 53) Both the Long- and Short-billed are so similar that it is impossible to distinguish them in flight. Both have a white cigar-shaped patch on their backs and very narrow trailing edges to wings. The Short-billed generally has paler secondaries and a barred white tail. The flight calls are different. Short-billed: a rapid mellow 'Kwetutu.' Long-billed: a high, sharp 'Keek' or 'pweek.'

Wilson's Snipe ws 18" (p. 53) When flushed, the zig-zag escaping flight is the best distinction from other waders. Prominent pale stripes on back are clearly visible in the field. Underwings dark gray. Flight call on take-off is an abrupt 'ca-ahtch.' The 'winnowing' display, produced by air vibrating the spread outer tail feathers, is only heard over its northern breeding territories.

Wilson's Phalarope ws 17" (p. 55) Pale gray with slightly darker, almost plain gray wings and large square white rump patch. Yellow toes project well beyond tail. Rather silent, sometimes softly grunts 'wurf.'

Red-necked Ph. ws 15" (p. 55) Darker gray with a well-marked but narrow, white wingstripe and white sides to rump. Flies fast with a flicking action. Flight call: a short nasal slightly throaty 'chep' or 'cherre.'

Red Ph. ws 17" (p. 55) Pale plain gray on mantle, while the Red-necked has a pale **V** on a darker back. Wings are longer and narrow, darker than the mantle with a well-marked white wingstripe. The rump is gray with just a little white at the edges. Flight call is a high, clear metallic 'pit' or 'piik.'

• **Gulls** *Laridae* 12 sp. Gregarious, long-winged, web-footed, opportunist seabirds, equally adept at flying, swimming and walking: scavengers and predators. This family is well-represented in Napa but does not breed within the county.

Larger gulls develop their full adult plumage in their 4th year; mostly white with pale to dark gray mantle and wing. Head white in br. plumage; smaller species have black hoods. The larger species have more or less mottled brown, dirty-looking heads in nbr. dress. Strong yellow bill in most species; some have a red spot or dark ring. Legs yellow or pink, changing with age.

The Western Gull breeds along the Pacific coast on suitable offshore rocks. Ring-billed and California breeds found inland but farther north and east. The really large gulls, but also Kittiwake and Bonaparte's, breed in higher latitudes up to the Arctic; there are no suitable places for them to breed in Napa County. Largest numbers are seen in the county from Sep.-Apr.

1st winter

ad nbr

ad br

ad nbr

1st winter

ad nbr

ad br

2nd winter

ad br

ad nbr

2nd winter

ad br

Mew Gull fW
Larus canus

L 43" Nests at ponds and rivers in boreal forests up to Alaska. From Sep. onwards, a common winter visitor along the coast. Many come inland to feed but never too far from the coast, visiting garbage dumps and, after heavy rain, flooded fields and pastures. Some remain for a while in the marshes. Very similar to the Ring-billed Gull in all plumages, so invariably it's hard to differentiate. Mews are slightly smaller and darker gray on mantle and wings; ad. have dark eyes, shorter legs and the yellow bill is thinner. In nbr. period, the faint dark bill ring is not as distinctive as the Ring-billed Gull's. Voices of both are very similar and higher pitched than Western Gulls'.

Ring-billed Gull cW, xSnbr
Larus delawarensis

L 17½" Together with the California, one of the most common and frequently seen gull in the county. When standing beside a Mew Gull the longer legs and paler back and wings are striking. The iris is pale when ad. and the bill is well-marked with a black ring. In their third winter they have full adult plumage like the Mew Gull. Before that, it can be confusing when comparing them to Mews. Generally, Ring-billeds are paler in all plumages, especially in their first winter: their bill is stouter with a bold black tip. In nbr. period the ad. has only faint streaks on the nape. In my opinion Ring-billeds have a less friendly expression than Mew Gulls.

◁ **2nd winter:** They resemble a 3rd winter Herring Gull and 1st winter Ring-billed. Though not easy to separate them, this can be done by the size and shape of their bills.

California Gull cW, rSnbr
Larus californicus

L 21" California has many gulls listed but only three breeding species. The California Gull is one of them, with a limited population in the Great Basin. Otherwise they breed more inland, from Utah up to northern Canada. Larger than the similarly yellow-legged Ring-billed but smaller than the pink-legged Western and Herring Gulls. Adults have dark eyes and red and black marks on their yellow bill. Darker mantles than the Ring-billed but paler than the larger, bulkier Western Gull. In flight they show extensive black wingtips and are relatively long-winged. Full ad. plumage after three years. Call is scratchy, hoarser and deeper than Ring-billed's.

Herring Gull cW, rSnbr
Larus argentatus

L 25" Cosmopolitan in northern hemisphere: no other gull has such a complicated and wide breeding distribution. Large, with a pale back, pale iris, large stout bill with a red mark, and pink legs. In nbr. plumage the head is mottled down the neck to the mantle. Juvenile birds are rather dark and it takes three years to acquire ad. plumage. More coastal than the California Gull; large numbers visit inland disposal sites, flying back to the bay to roost at night. Often seen mixing with other gulls in the tidal marshes. Call is a clear 'Kyow' and 'gag-ag-gag.'

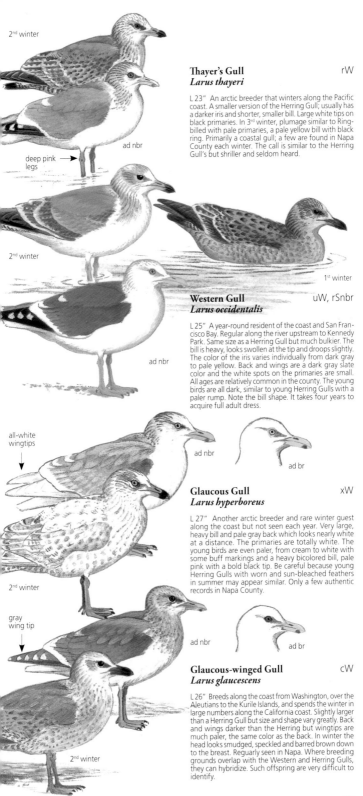

2nd winter

Thayer's Gull   rW
Larus thayeri

L 23" An arctic breeder that winters along the Pacific coast. A smaller version of the Herring Gull; usually has a darker iris and shorter, smaller bill. Large white tips on black primaries. In 3rd winter, plumage similar to Ring-billed with pale primaries, a pale yellow bill with black ring. Primarily a coastal gull; a few are found in Napa County each winter. The call is similar to the Herring Gull's but shriller and seldom heard.

ad nbr

deep pink legs

2nd winter

1st winter

Western Gull   uW, rSnbr
Larus occidentalis

L 25" A year-round resident of the coast and San Francisco Bay. Regular along the river upstream to Kennedy Park. Same size as a Herring Gull but much bulkier. The bill is heavy, looks swollen at the tip and droops slightly. The color of the iris varies individually from dark gray to pale yellow. Back and wings are a dark gray slate color and the white spots on the primaries are small. All ages are relatively common in the county. The young birds are all dark, similar to young Herring Gulls with a paler rump. Note the bill shape. It takes four years to acquire full adult dress.

ad nbr

all-white wingtips

ad nbr

ad br

Glaucous Gull   xW
Larus hyperboreus

L 27" Another arctic breeder and rare winter guest along the coast but not seen each year. Very large, heavy bill and pale gray back which looks nearly white at a distance. The primaries are totally white. The young birds are even paler, from cream to white with some buff markings and a heavy bicolored bill, pale pink with a bold black tip. Be careful because young Herring Gulls with worn and sun-bleached feathers in summer may appear similar. Only a few authentic records in Napa County.

2nd winter

gray wing tip

ad nbr

ad br

Glaucous-winged Gull   cW
Larus glaucescens

L 26" Breeds along the coast from Washington, over the Aleutians to the Kurile Islands, and spends the winter in large numbers along the California coast. Slightly larger than a Herring Gull but size and shape vary greatly. Back and wings darker than the Herring but wingtips are much paler, the same color as the back. In winter the head looks smudged, speckled and barred brown down to the breast. Regularly seen in Napa. Where breeding grounds overlap with the Western and Herring Gulls, they can hybridize. Such offspring are very difficult to identify.

2nd winter

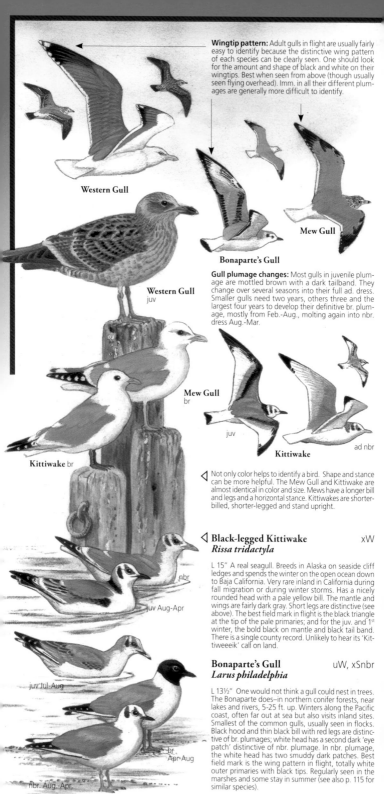

Wingtip pattern: Adult gulls in flight are usually fairly easy to identify because the distinctive wing pattern of each species can be clearly seen. One should look for the amount and shape of black and white on their wingtips. Best when seen from above (though usually seen flying overhead). Imm. in all their different plumages are generally more difficult to identify.

Western Gull

Mew Gull

Bonaparte's Gull

Western Gull
juv

Gull plumage changes: Most gulls in juvenile plumage are mottled brown with a dark tailband. They change over several seasons into their full ad. dress. Smaller gulls need two years, others three and the largest four years to develop their definitive br. plumage, mostly from Feb.-Aug., molting again into nbr. dress Aug.-Mar.

Mew Gull
br

Kittiwake br

juv

Kittiwake

ad nbr

◁ Not only color helps to identify a bird. Shape and stance can be more helpful. The Mew Gull and Kittiwake are almost identical in color and size. Mews have a longer bill and legs and a horizontal stance. Kittiwakes are shorter-billed, shorter-legged and stand upright.

nbr

juv Aug-Apr

juv Jul-Aug

br
Apr-Aug

nbr. Aug.-Apr.

◁ **Black-legged Kittiwake**   xW
Rissa tridactyla

L 15" A real seagull. Breeds in Alaska on seaside cliff ledges and spends the winter on the open ocean down to Baja California. Very rare inland in California during fall migration or during winter storms. Has a nicely rounded head with a pale yellow bill. The mantle and wings are fairly dark gray. Short legs are distinctive (see above). The best field mark in flight is the black triangle at the tip of the pale primaries; and for the juv. and 1st winter, the bold black on mantle and black tail band. There is a single county record. Unlikely to hear its 'Kittiweeeik' call on land.

Bonaparte's Gull   uW, xSnbr
Larus philadelphia

L 13½" One would not think a gull could nest in trees. The Bonaparte does–in northern conifer forests, near lakes and rivers, 5-25 ft. up. Winters along the Pacific coast, often far out at sea but also visits inland sites. Smallest of the common gulls, usually seen in flocks. Black hood and thin black bill with red legs are distinctive of br. plumages; white head has a second dark 'eye patch' distinctive of nbr. plumage. In nbr. plumage, the white head has two smuddy dark patches. Best field mark is the wing pattern in flight, totally white outer primaries with black tips. Regularly seen in the marshes and some stay in summer (see also p. 115 for similar species).

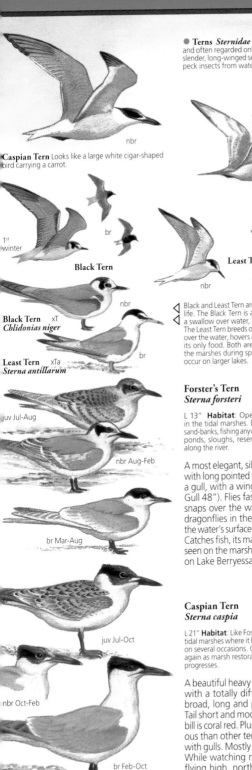

● Terns *Sternidae* 6 sp. Closely allied to the gulls and often regarded only as a sub-family. Very elegant, slender, long-winged seabirds. Catch fish by diving and peck insects from water's surface.

nbr

Caspian Tern Looks like a large white cigar-shaped bird carrying a carrot.

br

nbr

Forster's Tern Most elegant in flight, often calling a busy 'Kerrr' or shrill 'Kit,Kit.'

1st winter

br

Least Tern

Black Tern

nbr

nbr

Black Tern xT
Chlidonias niger

br

Least Tern xTa
Sterna antillarum

◁◁ Black and Least Tern are totally different in their way of life. The Black Tern is an inland marsh bird, flying like a swallow over water, pecking food from the surface. The Least Tern breeds on sandy beaches, flies a few feet over the water, hovers and plunges down to catch fish, its only food. Both are rare visitors, generally seen in the marshes during spring or early summer but could occur on larger lakes.

juv Jul-Aug

nbr Aug-Feb

br Mar-Aug

Forster's Tern   lfS
Sterna forsteri

L 13" **Habitat**: Open waters in the tidal marshes. Breeds on sand-banks, fishing anywhere—salt ponds, sloughs, reservoirs and along the river.

A most elegant, silvery white waterside bird with long pointed wings. Much smaller than a gull, with a wingspan of 31" (Ring-billed Gull 48"). Flies fast with quick, sharp wing snaps over the water; often seen chasing dragonflies in the air or pecking one from the water's surface without wetting a feather. Catches fish, its main food, by diving. Mostly seen on the marshes but has been observed on Lake Berryessa.

juv Jul-Oct

Caspian Tern   fSnb
Sterna caspia

L 21" **Habitat**: Like Foster's Tern, tidal marshes where it has nested on several occasions. Could nest again as marsh restoration work progresses.

nbr Oct-Feb

A beautiful heavy tern, the size of a gull but with a totally different shape. Wings are broad, long and pointed (wingspan 50"). Tail short and moderately forked. The stout bill is coral red. Plunges for fish. Less gregarious than other terns but often in company with gulls. Mostly seen in the tidal marshes. While watching magpies I observed three flying high, northeast over Blue Ridge at Lake Berryessa.

br Feb-Oct

Pigeons and Doves *Columbidae* 3 sp. There are 14 sp. on the U.S. list, 10 in California, and 3 in Napa. Pastel-colored grays or browns. Small heads, short bills and legs, heavy rounded fleshy bodies, strong direct flight.

Band-tailed Pigeon   iuP
Columba fasciata

L 14½" **Habitat**: Oak, conifer and mixed forests. Madrone trees are important as a source of food. Prefers to nest in Douglas fir or Redwood stands.

Heavier (13 oz.) than a street pigeon (9 oz.). Beautifully colored in pastel grays, pinkish hue on breast, yellow bill and feet. The double-noted cooing 'hu-whoo' is often mistaken for an owl's call. In pairs during the breeding season, in winter often in large flocks in search of oak mast and madrone crop. Erratic in their distribution, often absent where once common.

Plumage variations are possible, but it's all the same feral species.

Rock Pigeon   cP
Columba livia

L 12½" There is no real difference between a pigeon and a dove. The Rock Pigeon is an introduced species now found throughout the world. The original wild birds were bluish gray with black bars as illustrated here. In Napa there are no really wild populations; they always breed on buildings.

Mourning Dove   cP
Zenaida macroura

L 12" **Habitat**: Everywhere except deep woodland. Prefers dry open habitats, suburban, agricultural or open woods. Often seen on roadsides. Needs trees or bushes to nest.

An elegant bird. With its long tail it is not much shorter than a pigeon, but much smaller, weighing only 4.2 oz. Forages on the ground in search of seeds. When 'bursting' up in front of you, the white edges of their spade-shaped tail are distinctive. Often seen on overhead roadside wires. The mournful cooing 'coowAAh cooo coo coo' gave the birds their name.

62

hovering

diving

● **Kingfishers** *Alcedinidae* 1 sp. There are 92 species worldwide from tiny to large (4"-18") and all are similarly built and very colorful. Only one species is common throughout the U.S. An additional two species inhabit parts of Texas and Arizona.

uP

Belted Kingfisher
Ceryle alcyon

L 13" **Habitat**: Streams, rivers, lakes, wherever clear water runs and fish are plentiful. Needs a vertical bank, even far from water, to dig its 3-6 ft. deep nest chamber.

Belteds breed on the river in the city of Napa. A spectacular bird; large, noisy and showy. They are solitary and cannot tolerate others in their territory, except a mate in breeding season. Always using the same perch overlooking water, one just has to wait for its return while preparing the camera.

● **Cuckoos** *Cuculidae* 2 sp. American cuckoos are not brood parasites like most of the Old World species. Observing a pheasant-like Roadrunner, who would think it was a cuckoo? (See also p. 116.)

Familiar to everyone from cartoons and jokes about their amusing behavior and unbelievable postures. The bird running fast, catching an even faster lizard, is well known. Watching them in nature is a great pleasure.

rP

Greater Roadrunner
Geococcyx californicus

L 23" **Habitat**: Dry, open brush country, chaparral, rocky pine-oak foothills, abandoned farmland. Need dense, low trees or shrubby thickets for nesting.

A very elusive bird in Napa County; it's at the northwestern limit of its regular distribution. In spite of making a great effort I was not successful in observing them inside the county. Since they are very quiet, I didn't even hear one. They can fly but usually run away to hide or catch food: lizards, snakes, rodents, large insects and some birds.

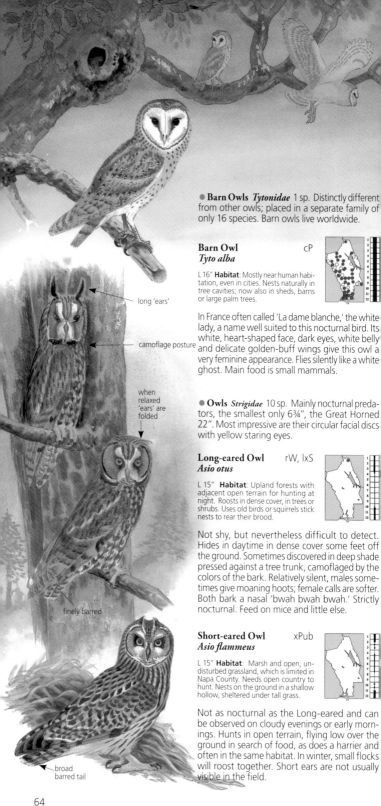

long 'ears'

camouflage posture

when relaxed 'ears' are folded

finely barred

broad barred tail

● **Barn Owls** *Tytonidae* 1 sp. Distinctly different from other owls; placed in a separate family of only 16 species. Barn owls live worldwide.

Barn Owl
Tyto alba

cP

L 16" **Habitat**: Mostly near human habitation, even in cities. Nests naturally in tree cavities; now also in sheds, barns or large palm trees.

In France often called 'La dame blanche,' the white lady, a name well suited to this nocturnal bird. Its white, heart-shaped face, dark eyes, white belly and delicate golden-buff wings give this owl a very feminine appearance. Flies silently like a white ghost. Main food is small mammals.

● **Owls** *Strigidae* 10 sp. Mainly nocturnal predators, the smallest only 6¾", the Great Horned 22". Most impressive are their circular facial discs with yellow staring eyes.

Long-eared Owl
Asio otus

rW, lxS

L 15" **Habitat**: Upland forests with adjacent open terrain for hunting at night. Roosts in dense cover, in trees or shrubs. Uses old birds or squirrels stick nests to rear their brood.

Not shy, but nevertheless difficult to detect. Hides in daytime in dense cover some feet off the ground. Sometimes discovered in deep shade pressed against a tree trunk, camoflaged by the colors of the bark. Relatively silent, males sometimes give moaning hoots; female calls are softer. Both bark a nasal 'bwah bwah bwah.' Strictly nocturnal. Feed on mice and little else.

Short-eared Owl
Asio flammeus

xPub

L 15" **Habitat**: Marsh and open, undisturbed grassland, which is limited in Napa County. Needs open country to hunt. Nests on the ground in a shallow hollow, sheltered under tall grass.

Not as nocturnal as the Long-eared and can be observed on cloudy evenings or early mornings. Hunts open terrain, flying low over the ground in search of food, as does a harrier and often in the same habitat. In winter, small flocks will roost together. Short ears are not usually visible in the field.

cP

Great Horned Owl
Bubo virginianus

L 22" **Habitat**: Found in any habitat, from the marshes to farmland to redwood forests. Hunts in vineyards and even town streets. Uses old nests of larger hawks to breed.

The largest and most powerful of all the owls–a magnificent wild creature. Found nearly everywhere. Nocturnal in its habits but will often hunt in the late afternoon, especially on cloudy days and when rearing a brood. Takes anything worthwhile catching; rabbits, squirrels, mice or large insects, but also cats and hawks. Voice: deep hoots and nasal barkings.

uP

Spotted Owl ▷
Strix occidentalis

L 17½" **Habitat**: Undisturbed old-growth redwood and mixed forest canyons. Nests in natural cavities in trees in well-shaded forests.

A national treasure; all efforts should be taken to preserve the Napa population and its habitat. Human presence is not too disturbing but human activities could be fatal. Very territorial, their nest and roosting sites are usually more than a mile apart. Strictly nocturnal, in daytime roosts high in the shade of a dense tree against the tree trunk. At night hunts on the forest floor. In Napa their most important prey is the Dusky-footed Woodrat. Their call is a deep barking 'huh…hoo-hooh' often heard in chorus. Also has a terrifying whistle. Female's call is higher. Voices are easy to imitate.

uP, ?S

Barred Owl ▷
Strix varia

L 21" Napa ornithologists are afraid that this owl will establish itself in the county. Larger than the Spotted, they could be a strong competitor for nesting and hunting territories, or even worse, could hybridize. During field work for this book I sketched an owl which I thought was a Spotted but analyzing the drawing in the evening, was sure we had found a Barred Owl. It had responded to whistling. Nothing can be done about this invader. Perhaps they can live side by side like *Strix* species do in other parts of the world.

Like the **Kestrel**, (p. 44), the **Pygmy Owl** has false eyes on its nape.

Old Hairy Woodpecker holes are often used by this owl for nesting.

Pygmys are very fierce daytime hunters of small birds up to their own size.

juv

Northern Pygmy Owl
Glaucidium gnoma   uP

L 6¾" **Habitat:** All kinds of open woodland with trees and bushes: oak canyons, forest edges, clearings in Douglas fir-Madrone woods, chaparral. Nests in tree holes.

The smallest breeding owl in the county, and the only one that hunts solely during daylight since their main prey is birds. Small birds react violently to a Pygmy's presence. Imitating the owl's whistle, 'poip,' can provoke great consternation amongst small birds, and the owl itself will react. Other hidden birds might suddenly appear. A pair of Pygmys occupies a large territory and will chase away any intruder of their own kind.

Northern Saw-whet Owl
Aegolius acadicus   rp

L 10" **Habitat:** Mixed upland forests, but most numerous in conifer stands. Usually nests in old Flicker or Pileated Woodpecker holes, and therefore depends on those species. Accepts nest boxes.

Seldom seen rare owl; strictly nocturnal in all its activities. Usually located through their calls, it is quite easy to imitate the whistle to which they will react. Large-headed, with a typical white V on its face. The young are very distinctive in rich chocolate-brown colors.

brown

Western Screech Owl
Otus kennicottii   cP

L 8½" **Habitat:** All over the county in suitably dry habitats. Likes old orchards, rural residential areas, only absent from the marshes and the city of Napa. Breeds and roosts in natural cavities and accepts nest boxes.

As illustrated on the map, the most widespread and also most common owl. Strictly nocturnal and generally overlooked since they roost in cavities during the day. Sometimes seen against a tree trunk, where their colors conceal them and they merge with the bark. Only their trills and whistle at night tell you they are around. Variable in color, as shown. Fledglings will leave their hole before they can fly properly, just small fluffy gray balls with staring yellow eyes.

gray

Flammulated Owl
Otus flammeolus   xTa

L 6¾" A tiny owl, weighing only 2.1 oz. with rather long broad wings. Nocturnal like the Screech Owl they resemble, except for their black eyes. There is also a gray morph which always has some rufous flash on the face. A rare passage migrant and surely overlooked. During migration they do not call and would pass unnoticed.

There is a relationship between Burrowing Owls and ground squirrels. Owls use their burrows to rest and breed, preferring abandoned burrows. Normally Burrowing Owls live in loose colonies. However, the bird is so rare in Napa, it's possible it no longer breeds in the county; only single pairs or solitary birds have been observed.

rW **Burrowing Owl**
Athene cunicularia

L 9½" Open grassland is the natural habitat for this terrestrial owl. Most active in early morning or late afternoon, when they hunt small rodents. We searched several locations where they are known to breed but failed to see any. They could still be in the north of Napa County.

● **Goatsuckers** *Caprimulgidae* 3 sp. A peculiar name for a bird family. Country people thought they sucked milk with their wide gape, when in reality they were catching insects around the sleeping goats.

xW, uS **Common Poorwill**
Phalaenoptilus nuttallii

L 7¾ **Habitat:** Rough chaparral slopes and similar dry ground with boulders and scattered bushes. Rests and nests on the ground.

A mysterious bird, some rest in the county during cold winter days and have been found at the Palisades hibernating, like marmots. In flight they resemble big moths, and moths are a major part of their diet. Voice: a mellow whistle 'poorWILL.'

Kestrel p. 44
ws 22"

Lesser Night
ws 22"

ws 24" **Common Nighthawk**

xTs **Common Nighthawk**
Chordeiles minor

L 91/2" A rare early summer visitor. I saw one at the northern end of Lake Berryessa on May 4, 2005, and first thought it was a kestrel. It flew high over some treetops, obviously catching insects in late afternoon. During the day mostly roosts on the ground or lengthwise on a branch.

xT **Lesser Nighthawk**
Chordeiles acutipennis

L 9" Very similar to Common Nighthawk. The white bar in the primaries is closer to the wingtip in the Lesser. Its flight style is similar; however, unlike the Common, it does not call in flight. Their size is little help. The summer range extends into the Sacramento Valley. There is one uncertain Napa record.

White-throated   Black Swift   Vaux's

● **Swifts** *Apodidae* 3 sp. Born to fly; the most aerial of all birds, whose long narrow sickle-shaped wings adapt them to very fast flight and feeding on flying insects. They cannot perch with their short legs; just cling to cliffs or tree trunks.

xW, uS

White-throated Swift
Aeronautes saxatalis

L 6½" ws 15" **Habitat**: Cliffs and canyons, ridges and high mountains. Nests in crevices in cliffs, on large bridges, also on Monticello Dam.

A resident, becoming rare in winter. Its clean white throat and belly stripe are diagnostic and make an otherwise wholly black bird look much bigger. I watched them on the top of Mount St. Helena, circling around, almost silent, but down on the Pallisades heard their noisy, shrill and machine-like call 'Ki Ki Ki Kir Kir Kir Kiirr.'

Black Swift   ixT
Cypseloides niger

L 7¼" ws 18" A large, all-black swift with a slightly forked tail. Has a particularly local and coastal distribution. A migrant and could pass through Napa in spring and fall. Flies in small groups or mixes with the much smaller Vaux's Swift. Their wingbeats are leisurely and they often soar.

Vaux's Swift   uTs, rTa
Chaetura vauxi

L 4¾" ws 12" Like a cigar on wings. Regularly seen in the county, and it's difficult to understand why they don't breed here. In nearby Healdsburg, they use a deserted chimney as an autumn roosting site where several thousand birds gather together. They nest in burnt-out conifer trees.

● **Hummingbirds** *Trochilidae* 6 sp. A purely American family of 328 species: tiny, long-billed, mostly short-tailed birds with over-developed wings for hovering in flight, to suck nectar from flowers and to catch small flying insects.

Costa's Hummingbird   xTS
Calypte costae

L 3½" A desert lover of California and a very early breeder from Jan. onwards. A few, mostly males, can over-fly their normal breeding haunts and occur at a Napa feeder, often staying a long time. Females are more difficult to recognize.

Calliope Hummingbird   rTS
Stellula calliope

L 3¼" Their preferred habitat is meadow edges of mountain conifer forest but also riparian thickets. The tiniest of U.S. hummingbirds, even if very short-tailed. Male has a distinctive streaky rose gorget and the female is pale buff below.

sub ad ♂   ad ♂

The most striking feature of all humming-birds is their brilliant iridescent plumage. As shown here, similar head and gorget colors can change in different light or at whatever angles you view the bird. Sub ad. males only have a little red, such as this Anna's, slowly molting into full bright ad. plumage. Adult females have some red on throat.

xWbr, cP **Anna's Hummingbird**
Calypte anna

L 4" **Habitat**: Common all year round in open woodland, chaparral, parks and gardens with flowering vegetation. Breeds in mid-Jan. till the end of Jun.

The most familiar hummer. Readily visits feeding ▷ stations. Often seen perched on an exposed dead twig, preening and overlooking the feeding territory, chasing away any intruder. Bill proportionately short compared with similar Black-chinned. Females of both species are very similar; Black-chinned are smaller, more delicately formed, longer billed. In Jan. male, *above*, courts the female. Once the eggs are laid the male takes no interest in the family, which is reared by the female alone.

← often looks nearly black

ad. ♂

♂

♀

xTS **Black-chinned Hummingbird**
Archilochus alexandri

L 3¾" **Habitat**: Lowlands, wooded canyons ▷ and alongside streams for nesting, but there is no authentic breeding record in Napa County. Males summer high up on sunny canyon sides.

Very rare and there are only a few records in Napa. Perhaps some are overlooked since they are so similar to the more robust Anna's. Look for the white collar, longer bill and paler underside. Spreads and flips tail, as though pumping, when hovering. A migratory species but some winter in California.

uS **Allen's Hummingbird**
Selasphorus sasin

L 3¾" **Habitat**: Chaparral and riparian woods, ▷ also suburbs and may have benefited from the increased number of hummingbird feeders and exotic eucalyptus trees.

A very early migrant, arriving in late winter. There is no problem distinguishing them from the other hummers except the Rufous, which is a passage migrant and breeds farther north. Allen's males have green backs. The outer tail feathers are very narrow and pointed but are very difficult to see in the field.

uT **Rufous Hummingbird** ▷
Selasphorus rufus

L 3¾" Very common north of California but in Napa only seen during their migration in Mar. and Apr. The males have bright rufous backs with traces of green. The female is indistinguishable from the Allen's in the field. Rufous have relatively longer wings compared to Allen's.

69

Acorn

juv Jul-Nov

ad

Lewis's

juv Jul-Mar

♀ has a white throat

Mated pairs of Woodpeckers are territorial, except the Acorn, which lives all year round in complicated family groups of a dozen or more members to protect their granaries and nest sites.

● **Woodpeckers** *Picidae* 12 sp. of which, 6 breed in Napa. Highly adapted birds, with strong claws, short legs and stiff tail feathers which enable them to climb tree trunks. Strong chisel-shaped bills to search for food and excavate their nesting holes.

Acorn Woodpecker   cP
Melanerpes formicivorus

Habitat: Mixed and open oak woods but practically everywhere oaks grow and there are dead trees, even on urban edges, where they use telephone poles as their granaries.

L 9" The most familiar and widespread woodpecker in Napa, found throughout the county except the marshes; black, with a clown-like face and red cap. In flight the large white rump and broad white wing patches are distinctive. Acorns, their main food, provide up to 50% of their diet. Stored in specially drilled holes, called granaries, acorns provide their basic energy in winter. Expert fly catchers, they frequently sally from treetops to catch insects, their most important food during spring and the breeding season.

Lewis's Woodpecker   luW, xSnbr
Melanerpes lewis

L 10¾" Their preferred habitat is dry open country with scattered oaks and pines in the northern part of the county. When flying slowly between trees, looks more like a small crow than a woodpecker. At a distance, it's slate black with a gray collar. Close up, the wine-red face, pink belly and green sheen on back makes the bird look more colorful. In winter they usually live in loose flocks and wander around in their preferred habitat but can be found again in the same trees, especially when acorns are abundant. Arrive generally in Nov. and remain all winter until Apr., then suddenly disappear. Some have been observed in summer but never found breeding. Mostly silent; I did not hear one calling.

◁ **Yellow-bellied Sapsucker**   xW
Sphyrapicus varius

L 8½" A stranger from Canada, where they live in mixed coniferous forests. Napa is far out of its way from the normal southeastern winter quarters. There is only one record in the county. A very quiet and retiring bird and possibly overlooked when it has found its way to Napa. Resembles larger Nuttall's Woodpecker; has a longish white wing stripe and rump patch visible in flight. In late fall young birds are mottled with some red on the crown.

Red-naped Sapsucker
Sphyrapicus nuchalis

L 8½" The western counterpart of the Yellow-bellied, and identical except for the larger red throat patch and red spot on the nape. A few pairs breed in California. No county records but expected to appear. They winter farther south, mostly in Mexico. To separate the two sapsuckers in the field is not easy, and it's difficult to get a good view of their head pattern.

Yellow-bellied   Red-naped   Red-breasted

Sapsucker females are all similar and often variable in color, which makes their identification difficult.

uW

Red-breasted Sapsucker
Sphyrapicus ruber

L 8½" The third of the sapsucker group. Breeds in the California mountains but prefers to overwinter in humid lowlands with tall trees. The sapsucker most likely to be seen in the county. With its red head, the male is easy to identify, but worn California females can resemble female Red-naped, though throat and breast are red. The young are like the Yellow-bellied but overall much darker.

xW   ♂

Williamson's Sapsucker
Sphyrapicus thyroides

L 9" A common California resident of the higher mountains where they live in pine forests. In winter occasionally move to lowlands and some reach Napa County. Sexes are entirely different. The male resembles an all-black Red-naped with a large white wing panel. The female has the colors of a flicker. Both show a large white rump when flying away, and a yellow belly, brighter than the Yellow-bellied Sapsucker.

juvenile

The juvenile *Melanerpes* Woodpeckers and and Sapsuckers have no red on their heads and are distinctly different in color from their parents. Juvenile *Picoides* Woodpeckers in general resemble adults but have more red on the crown until mid Aug. After molting, they start to wander (see next page).

xW

White-headed Woodpecker
Picoides albolarvatus

no red

L 9¼" Uncommon in the Coast Range, but common in the Sierra Nevada, where they live in mature coniferous forests. In winter, when their main food–seeds of Sugar and Ponderosa Pines–are in short supply, they move casually to lower altitudes. Similar in habits and size to the common Hairy Woodpecker, but distinctly different in all-black plumage with white head, unique amongst woodpeckers. The white wing patch is most obvious in flight. Only the male has a red patch on the nape, which is the rule in this genus. There is one Napa County record.

71

Nuttall's are acrobatic when searching for food on smaller branches, frequently hanging upside down, poking energetically into crevices like titmice.

Nuttall's Woodpecker cP
Picoides nuttallii

L 7½" **Habitat**: Oak groves, mixed tree growth, riparian woodland but also in suburbs or orchards, preferably near watercourses. Nest-hole in tree trunks 2-60 ft. up.

Only found in California as a breeding bird, and fairly common in the lower parts of Napa County but mostly absent from the higher elevations. In size between the Downy and Hairy; a more delicate shape with a distinctive barred back. The red hind crown in the male shows up more than in the other two species.

Hairy Woodpecker fP
Picoides villosus

L 9¼" **Habitat**: Locally in wooded foothills with large mature trees. Has a preference for Douglas fir and redwood. Nesthole in tree trunks or large limbs 3-55 ft. up.

A common woodpecker found throughout North America. The local Pacific subspecies has gray-brown underparts and a few white wing spots but they are variable in color and look smudged. The whitish patch on its back, similar to the much smaller Downy, is distinctive. Lengthy, fast drumming with its bill. The Nuttall's is much slower.

Downy Woodpecker fP
Picoides pubescens

L 7¼" **Habitat**: Open moist woodland, often along streams where alder and willow grow. Rarely in upland hardwoods. Nest-hole in dead branches or stubs. Entrance hole only 1¼" in diameter.

The most silent and secretive of the resident woodpeckers, very similar to the Hairy but much smaller; a real dwarf with short body and puppet-like appearance. Often forages on small twigs and even weed stems in search of insects. Drums briefly and slowly on a resounding dead branch.

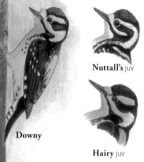

All three youngsters in this group resemble their parents with the same basic black-and-white pattern. Generally the plumage looks softer and fluffier, the black areas are duller and the underparts darker. Both sexes have a red crown unlike the adults. The male's can be speckled with white or gray, and female's is less intense and patchy. In young Downy females there can be just a few red feathers and sometimes none. This red crown varies considerably and can look yellowish; is never as red as in the adult male's red nape patch.

Young *Picoides* woodpeckers are already very aggressive with each other in the nest. When fledged they try to stay apart. As do their parents, they live solitary lives in winter and roost singly in their holes, which they make in autumn. They feed mostly on insects, some berries in fall and seeds in winter, but these are less important than for Acorn Woodpeckers.

Often work on old rotten stumps and fallen logs
in search of carpenter ants, larvae and wood-boring beetles,
their favorite food. Also eat wild fruit.

uP **Pileated Woodpecker**
Dryocopus pileatus

L 16½" **Habitat**: Mature, unbroken mixed and coniferous upland forests; also second growth forest with some
large trees. Nest in cavities in dead wood. Entrance hole
oval and over 4" high.

♂, ♀ red on crest
less extensive
and moustache
black

Generally seen alone, but paired birds keep loose contact in
their large territory all year round. Usually heard before seen.
Their loud maniacal call 'yucka yucka yucka' carries far. They
mark their territory by a slow but powerful drumming. The
best sign of their presence is the great square cornered holes
in decaying timber. From a distance, rotten trees resemble
honeycombs.

Yellow-shafted

♂

♀

Red-shafted

♂

Flickers are ground foragers, taking most of their food by
probing in the soil. Ants make up to 75% of their diet, which
includes termites, beetles and their larvae, spiders, and also
some fruit and berries.

cW, fS **Northern Flicker**
Colaptes auratus

L 13" **Habitat**: In all wooded areas but preferably oak
woodlands. Usually in forested hills during the breeding
season. Nesting cavity in partly dead wood with rather large
entrance hole (2-4"). Often makes several nest-holes.

The resident Red-shafted Flicker is common and widespread
across the county. In winter, easterly birds move in, often
hybrids with the Yellow-shafted. A rather large woodpecker
with a typically white rump, its undulating flight is distinctive
when flushed. Their call is a loud clear 'Kleeyah.' During spring
a ringing continuous 'wik-wik-wikwi' can be heard. The spring
call resembles that of the Pileated Woodpecker.

73

unbuttoned vest

cotton-white tufts, often exposed

short tail

- **Tyrant Flycatchers** *Tyrannidae* 14 sp. A very large, entirely American family. Large-headed, with broad-based bills and typically bristly whiskers. Most Northern American flycatchers look drab in worn plumage and are not easy to identify. All are migratory, overwintering from Mexico southwards, except the Black Phoebe which is sedentary, and the Say's Phoebe which winters in parts of California.

The long pointed wings of this Olive-sided are typical of most Tyrant Flycatchers. Perching upright on a dead branch near the treetop, watching for passing insects. After capture, returns to its observation post. Can use the same perch for weeks.

Olive-sided Flycatcher   uS
Contopus cooperi

L 7½" **Habitat**: Coniferous woodlands, favoring Douglas fir, often on forest edges. Nests on a horizontal branch up to 70 ft. high, usually in a conifer but, in the Bay Area, also in eucalyptus groves.

long

short tail

The Olive-sided is a long-distance migrant returning to Napa from its South American winter quarters after Apr. 20, and it lays eggs about the time of the summer solstice. The longest nesting period of all flycatchers, with five weeks from laying to fledgling. They are easy to identify: dark in appearance with a pale stripe running down the breast and white 'tufts' on the back. The frequently heard song 'Pe-Prebee' sounds like 'three beer' said quickly.

Western Wood Pewee   fS
Contopus sordidulus

L 6¼" **Habitat**: Borders of deciduous and mixed forests, open Savannah, chaparral slopes and also riparian woodland. Nests on large branches 15-30 ft. up in a tree.

long

Their scientific name, *sordidulus*, refers to their dusky colors, their best field mark. Larger and longer than the similar *Empidonax* flycatchers, with long pointed wings and narrow but not distinctive wing bars. Like the Olive-sided, catches flying insects, but prefers the lower canopy for hunting. On damp mornings will often hover over foliage to take insects. When perched, sits still without flicking its tail and is silent. The nasal 'pee yee' whistle can be heard especially when males defend their territory.

Willow Flycatcher   uT
Empidonax traillii

short

long tail

L 5¾" An uncommon fall migrant rarely seen during spring migration. In California, breeds along four southern rivers and in a few Sierra meadows. The California breeding population is endangered. On migration, single birds are likely to be seen in willow thickets along streams. Has a rather flat head and longer bill than other *Empidonax* species. The eye ring is very faint and sometimes absent; the tail is relatively long. The best field mark is their song, a sneezy 'Fitz-bew' but of no help in Napa since migrating birds rarely sing. Juveniles resemble a pewee but are smaller, shorter-billed and with a paler throat and belly.

short

long

Dusky Flycatcher rTS, xSt
Empidonax oberholseri

L 5¾" **Habitat**: A high-mountain bird, only found on Mount St. Helena above 3,800 ft. where brush and sugarpine meet, and at Haystack Mount Breeding has not been proved in either locality.

Identifying the small *Empidonax* flycatchers is not easy. The Dusky, a rare mountain dweller, is overall more gray-olive than the browner Willow; has a longer tail and neat rounded head. Most distinctive is the short stubby bill. The eye ring and both wing bars are clearly visible. Song: a repeated series of high 'chrip…grreep…quwerrp.' Call: a soft 'whit.'

Pacific-slope Flycatcher cS
Empidonax difficilis

L 5½" **Habitat**: Moist coniferous and mixed woods, shady steep-walled canyons and ravines. Usually in shady undergrowth. Nests behind loose bark, even on ledges of buildings and in forest road cuttings.

Most common on the western side of the county wherever there are moist shadowy woods, with a preference for bay and live oak or old stands of willows. Long-tailed but compact build, with a slightly crested crown. In general there is a yellowish tinge on the belly and throat but some adults are quite drab. The eye ring is broad and pointed at the rear. Song: unslurred 'suwheet' (see also p. 116).

ical
wagging

juv

Often perches on a gravel bank or on rocks in streams.

ad

Black Phoebe cP
Sayornis nigricans

L 7" **Habitat**: Never far from water, peferably streams; the surrounding vegetation is less important. They need mud to build their nest in the bank of a stream, under a bridge or in the eave of a building.

A common and well-known flycatcher. Usually found in the same place throughout the year, perching on low branches wagging its tail. Identification is easy; no other bird looks like it. Early in Mar. they start to build their cup-shaped mud nest and they seem to like human presence. There must be water nearby, even if only a trickling stream or dripping water pipe. Song: a rising high 'pee-wee.'

ad

Say's Phoebe uW
Sayornis saya

L 7½" Breeds in the dryer parts of Southern California, where it is resident, and in the east, where it is a summer visitor. The eastern visitors pass through Napa on their way to Mexico, where they overwinter, but some remain for the winter, generally on open farmland or golf courses. Closely resemble the Black Phoebe in their habits. Appear slightly larger with a pointed head; rather dull gray with a rufous belly. See the white-bellied Eastern Phoebe (p. 116), which has similar habits.

Western Kingbird
Tyrannus verticalis cS

L 8¾" **Habitat**: Any sunny open habitat: prairies, agricultural pasture land. The large untidy nest is built on a large limb, fencepost, building or similar site.

Usually seen alone, in pairs or small family groups. Perches upright on wires or fences, often along roadsides. Fiercely defends its territory against all intruders whether a small kestrel, a large Red-tailed Hawk or a cat, and chases them away. The neat, pale gray head, clean sulphur-yellow belly and black tail with white edges are unique. The small orange-red crown stripe is usually concealed.

Ash-throated Flycatcher
Myiarchus cinerascens cS

L 8¾" **Habitat**: Widely distributed in all native brushy woodland habitats, only avoids dense forests. Nests in natural cavities, old woodpecker holes or behind loose bark. Accepts nest boxes.

More secretive and not as outgoing as the Western Kingbird; prefers to perch in a tree not in the open. Most are alone or in pairs. Pale gray breast, darker gray on head and back and very light yellow, nearly white belly. Reddish edges in flight feathers and entire undertail. Slender in shape with a longish but broad tail and peaked head. Feeds mostly on insects but also berries.

● **Shrikes** *Laniidae* 2 sp. Songbirds with the habits of hawks. Strong bill with hooked tip. Spends long periods perched motionless on top of a bush or on wires on the lookout for prey.

Black wings and tail with white markings, most visible in flight. Mockingbird (p. 88) has similar pattern.

Loggerhead Shrike
Lanius ludovicianus uP

L 9" **Habitat**: Open areas with scattered perches in shrubs, trees, on fences or telephone lines. Pasture land and golf courses are most favored. Nests in isolated shrubs or trees with dense cover.

Their favorite habitat is regularly grazed pasture. They stay in the same areas for years but move away if grazing ceases and weeds and bushes take over the land. They need short grass in which to catch their prey of large insects and small rodents. Observation posts are important and can be a fencepost, a wire or a bush. Roadside telephone lines that cross their territory are ideal, and that is where to look for them.

Northern Shrike
Lanius excubitor xTa

L 10" Larger and paler than Loggerhead, with a narrower dark mask and more white above eyes. (Not illustrated.)

juv

ad

small

Ruby-crowned Kinglet

thick bill

rounded head

pointed

small

• **Vireos** *Vireonidae* 3 sp. Small chunky song-birds with stout, shrike-like hooked bills. Easily confused with warblers but are generally less active. The spectacled pattern around their eyes is typical.

◁ Ruby-crowned Kinglet (p. 90) and Hutton's Vireo are surprisingly similar. The vireo is more compact and has a much thicker bill. The best field mark is the Kinglet's dark area below the pale wing bar and also its voice. In winter when vireos join small birds' feeding parties, they can mix in the same flock with warblers and chickadees.

Hutton's Vireo   fP
Vireo huttoni

L 5" **Habitat**: Resident and common in oak woods, but mostly overlooked. Non-migratory and in extremely cold winters their population can drop drastically.

Closely associated with live oak throughout the year but also found in mixed deciduous forests and Douglas fir, especially at the end of the breeding season, which can start in Feb. and extends through Jul. The nest, a deep cup of lichens, plant down, fine grasses, hair and spiderwebs, is suspended from a forked twig. Both parents tend their brood. They glean their food, principally insects and spiders, from foliage. In winter they also take small fruits and some seeds.

Cassin's Vireo   fS
Vireo cassinii

L 5½" **Habitat**: Mixed forests. More of a generalist than the Hutton's. Shows a preference for upland dry oak or co-nifer stands but also breeds in riparian remnants of oak and bay.

Fairly common in the western hills of the county and easily distinguished from Hutton's by the bluish gray head with bold white 'spectacles.' However, before leaving for their winter quarters, the young birds, with their greenish-gray heads, resemble the Hutton's closely and are not easy to distinguish. Same habits as Hutton's, sometimes chase moths and butterflies, hovering like all vireos to catch insects from foliage; when conditions offer no choice, will eat berries or small seeds.

Warbling Vireo   fS
Vireo gilvus

L 5½" **Habitat**: Mature mixed hillside forests and deciduous woodland in the Valley. Absent from arid chaparral. Usually nests high in trees in a horizontal forked twig.

Well-named, they rank high among the Napa songsters. Their song resembles that of the Purple Finch, though more musical and rapid, and they are more often heard than seen. After the nice song, they have a rather harsh nasal 'meezh' call. It is the most warbler-like vireo with pale lores and eye stripe that create a blank expression. They prefer to stay in the upper canopy, gleaning insects and spiders underneath the foliage.

Napa's population of warbling vireos that breed in the upland forests remains stable, but in general, numbers in California are decreasing, perhaps due to cowbird parasitism. Destruction of habitat remains the greatest threat.

● **Jays and Crows** *Corvidae* 8 sp. A very successful, noisy and aggressive family. Gregarious, and territorial around nest during breeding season. (For two more jays, see p. 111.)

blue

Broad rounded wings, short tail, belly all blue. Looks dark in flight –especially the head.

Steller's Jay
Cyanocitta stelleri

cP

L 11½" **Habitat**: Most common in densely mixed mountain and hill forests. Prefers conifer stands of redwood and fir but also inhabits slopes with live oaks, particularly in autumn during oak mast.

Brilliant blue and black. Colors often show up more in the shade of the woods than in bright sunshine. Their presence is heard before they are seen. Varied calls but their 'shak shak shak' is heard most and carries far.

long   white

Flight similar to Steller's. Tail longer and pale back; light belly gives them a white 'rear end.'

Western Scrub Jay
Aphelocoma californica

cP

L 11½" **Habitat**: Wherever oaks grow, from the mountains to the Valley, wild country and suburban areas. Steller's and Scrubs often occur together in the same areas. The Scrub is the more common jay in the county.

Abundant and noisy. Their angry and rough 'check check, check-check' can be heard everywhere, as well as the rasping flight call 'Kwesh Kwesh.' Two together in a dense bush can utter soft warbling notes and a peculiar rolling 'burrr'.

long

Unmistakable, black and white, with a long tail. The bright yellow bill shows up well and is clearly visible at a distance.

Yellow-billed Magpie
Pica nuttalli

rP

L 16½" **Habitat**: Oak savannah on the east side of Lake Berryessa. Breeds in small colonies. Sometimes seen around ranches in fall and winter.

Gregarious, move in small flocks but very shy during breeding season, especially near their colony. Stay at a distance from the observer. In fall and winter, more confident and often bold. Their bulky nests, sometimes several in a tree, indicate their presence.

fan-shaped tail

Black-billed Magpie
Pica hudsonia

XP

L 19" Resident along the eastern California border. There are a few records of single birds in Napa County, possibly escaped caged birds, since they rarely wander. Slightly larger than the Yellow-billed, tail longer, bill black and smaller white shoulder patch.

American Crow
Corvus brachyrhynchos

cP

L 17½" **Habitat**: Found almost everywhere except in dense forests, with a preference for settled landscapes where food is abundant. Nests in trees or large shrubs. Outside the breeding season roosts in flocks at night.

Common and well known. Similar to the much larger raven for which they are often mistaken. Their familiar call is softer but still a harsh 'Caw! Caw! Cuaw!' Juveniles are less glossy and 'blue-eyed.'

wedge shaped tail

Like an all-black flying cross. Wingspan of 53" (crow 39", Red-tailed Hawk 49", Cormorant 52").

Common Raven
Corvus corax

fP

L 24" **Habitat**: Found all over the county. Very successful and slowly increasing. Takes advantage of human presence but breeds predominantly in the wilder uplands and also in the marshes. Nests in tall trees, cliffs and rocky outcrops.

The largest all-black bird in the county and the largest songbird worldwide. Flies heavily but often soars and in spring performs remarkable aerobatics–tumbling, flying upside-down, nose diving. Walks majestically.

Steller's Jay

juv.

ad

Scrub Jay

ad

juv

Black-billed Magpie

ad

Yellow-billed Magpie

ad

yellow varies

American Crow

ad

juv

juv blue eyes

Common Raven

ad

juv.. whitish belly

Tree Swallow   **Violet-Green**   juv

ad   juv   ad

Tree Swallow has dark cheeks. Violet-Green Swallow has white cheeks and white above eye.

On cool mornings, swallows of all species frequently gather, lining up on power or telephone wires like pearls on a string. They sit a short distance from each other 'warming up' for the day, doing their morning grooming.

Swallows are so agile and fly so fast that identification is often very difficult. Tree and Violet-Green Swallows are very similar in color and pattern. Violet-Green's white underside wraps onto side of rump.

● **Swallows** *Hirundinidae* 7 sp. Built for aerial life with long, pointed but broader wings than similar swifts (p. 68). Except for the Tree Swallow, which also eats berries, feed exclusively on flying insects.

Purple Martin   lrS
Progne subis

L 8" **Habitat**: Mixed chaparral and open conifer slopes, ridges with isolated Douglas fir and open meadows nearby. Nests in trees, in old woodpecker holes.

Large and long-winged, generally forages higher up than other swallows, over any open habitat, preferring ridges. Mostly seen in pairs or small flocks of 4-5 birds. Keeps away from settled areas, unlike in the eastern states. The only breeding martins I observed in Napa occupied old woodpecker holes in a telephone pole near a farmhouse surrounded by open meadows and pine-covered ridges.

Tree Swallow   irW, cS
Tachycineta bicolor

L 5¾" **Habitat**: Any open country, forages in large flocks over fields, meadows and water. Nests singly in tree cavities and accepts nest boxes, even when fixed to a fencepost.

Very common in Napa. Small flocks are present throughout winter in tidal marshes. Breeds all over the county, concentrating in Napa Valley; avoids higher elevations. Easily attracted to nest boxes that are erected for swallows and bluebirds in many vineyards. Starts breeding mid Apr. Two females might lay in the same nest.

Violet-Green Swallow   xW, cS
Tachycineta thalassina

L 5¼" **Habitat**: Mountain canyons and forests but avoids hard chaparral slopes and also tidal marshes. Nests in tree cavities and rock crevices but rarely in nest boxes. Begins to breed in May.

Similar to the Tree Swallow. They often forage together over open areas, usually near water. Smaller than the Tree Swallow, flies with faster wingbeats, glides less. Usually in small groups, breeding in loose colonies when possible, unlike the Tree Swallow, which is a solitary nester but forms large feeding flocks. Winters sporadically in the Napa marshes.

Bank
Swallow

Barn Swallow

Rough-winged

juv   ad

♂

juv

ad

ad

Cliff Swallow   cS
Petrochelidon pyrrhonota

L 5½ **Habitat**: Forages over open fields
and ponds, from the north to the marshes,
avoids densely vegetated upland. Nests
on manmade structures, under bridges
or house eaves.

A better name for them now might be cement
swallow. Apparently they have abandoned their
colonies on overhanging cliff ledges and build their
well-known gourd-shaped mud nests on manmade
structures, often in very large, crowded colonies
of up to 1,000 pairs. Highly migratory, first arrive
mid-Mar.; by end Sep. all have gone.

Barn Swallow   cS
Hirundo rustica

L 6¾" **Habitat**: Open farmland. Prior
to European settlement, they nested in
open caves, under overhanging rocks
but now as with the Cliff Swallow, only
use manmade structures.

They were named in England, where they breed
in stables and barns, as they do now in most
parts of North America. Napa birds usually stay
outside, building their cup-shaped mud nests
under bridges or house eaves. A swallow's nest
is still considered a lucky omen.

Northern   fS
Rough-winged Swallow
Stelgidopteryx serripennis

L 5½" **Habitat**: Forages near water in
any open country. Usually nests solitarily
in a burrow dug in steep sand or gravel
bank, crevices in cliffs, walls or buildings,
even far from water.

A widespread but not well known swallow. Has
benefited from human activity for nesting sites
like most swallows. Perhaps more common now
than formerly. Overall drab brown except for the
striking white undertail coverts against the dark
square tail. Juveniles have typically rusty bars in
dark earth-brown wings.

Bank Swallow   eS, xT
Riparia riparia

L 5¼" Probably still bred in Napa in 1930 but suitable habitats
no longer exist. A colonial nester needing vertical sandbanks,
natural or artificial, in which to dig their long nest tunnels.
Seldom seen far from water except on migration. Our smallest
swallow, with narrow, notched tail, dark underwings and a
broad breast band on clean white breast. Since 1930 there
have been 3 county records.

81

● **Titmice** *Paridae* 3 sp. Non-migratory, small, hardy, active, acrobatic insectivores that also feed on seeds year-round. There are 10 species in the U.S., of which 5 breed in California, 2 in Napa.

Chestnut-backed Chickadee fP
Poecile rufescens

L 4¾" **Habitat**: Common in coniferous and mixed forests, also in riparian woodland, upland live oak and even in suburbs with exotic conifers. Nests in a cavity it excavates in dead wood.

During the breeding season, from winter's end until Jul., pairs will hold a territory to raise their large brood of 5-9 chicks. Later, several families will group together with other small birds such as Hutton's Vireo, kinglets, nuthatches or warblers; the flock then roams in the woods and bushes in search of food, covering a wide area each day.

Mountain Chickadee xTa
Poecile gambeli

L 5¼" Breeds in conifers on the highest mountains and seldom leaves the breeding haunt. Only moves to lower elevations when circumstances are severe. There is a record of two on Mount St. Helena and perhaps there are others. When far from their normal range, they prefer to keep to higher elevations where there is very little birding during the colder winter months.

Oak Titmouse cP
Baeolophus inornatus

L 5¾" **Habitat**: Prefers oak woodland but also common in residential areas where oaks grow, and at edges of mixed forests with Douglas fir. Nests in cavities, accepts nest boxes.

Once called the Plain Titmouse, and without a crest it would look very plain. Not spectacular but a very interesting bird. A pair will keep a territory throughout the year, which is unusual for small birds. Their nest in a cavity or bird box is built mostly by the female; both parents rear the brood until they are independent. Readily comes to feeding stations; fond of suet and sunflower seeds.

● **Long-tailed Tits** *Aegithalidae* 1 sp. Only one species of this small family of 8 members occurs in the New World and is very common in Napa.

Bushtit cP
Psaltriparus minimus

L 4½" **Habitat**: Open oak woodland, mountain chaparral, mixed conifers, riparian groves and gardens with scrub and bushes. Nest is in a tree or shrub, suspended from a forked twig.

With longish tail and weighing only 0.19 oz., the lightest songbird (Kinglet 4", 0.21 oz.). Bushtits live all year in flocks of about 25-40 members. Hyperactive, bouncing throughout the bushes, examining everything in search of aphids and small insects. They huddle together in cold weather to reduce heat loss. Their nest is a nicely woven, elongated hanging pouch. Despite their small size they defend their nest aggressively against all predators. Both parents incubate, and single males will often help to rear the brood.

Females have pale, staring eyes; males dark eyes. Brown tone on head varies greatly, and males can have darker cheeks

82

Nuthatches have short rounded wings and a white pattern in the short square tail, distinctive when flying away. The three species are difficult to seperate in flight.

♂

♀

♂

♀

ad

Pygmys are more social than other nuthatches and in winter often stay in a small flock together. During the breeding season an additional adult may help to rear the brood.

● **Nuthatches** *Sittidae* 3 sp. Small, compact, active birds with a jerky gait. No other birds habitually descend trees head down. They feed on invertebrates, seeds and nuts. Hole nesters.

White-breasted Nuthatch cP
Sitta carolinensis

L 5¾" **Habitat**: Common in all mature, leafy woods across the county; visits gardens. Pairs keep a permanent territory during the year. Nests in natural cavity, and accepts nest boxes.

The largest, most widespread North American nuthatch and also the most common in Napa. In winter visits bird feeders for suet and sunflower seeds. Visits to the feeder are often very quick; picking up a seed, flying away to store it and returning. Once established at a feeder, a pair will chase away any other nuthatch. Noisy. Pacific coast birds have their own dialect.

Red-breasted Nuthatch iuW, rS
Sitta canadensis

L 4½" **Habitat**: Prefers upland coniferous but also mixed oak and Douglas fir woods on steep slopes. Excavates its own nest cavity.

Usually solitary, and an irregular breeder in Napa County. I heard and saw only one on the steep slope of Mount St. Helena; a somewhat nasal but soft call: 'ennk ennk ennk.' Its breast was rather pale but the cap dark, so I thought it was a male. He seemed to be quite tame and I watched him up close while he was pecking in soft rotten wood.

Pygmy Nuthatch fW, uS
Sitta pygmaea

L 4¼" **Habitat**: Old-growth ponderosa pine but also Douglas fir forests with dying and decaying trees. Nests high up in a cavity, excavated or enlarged by the bird.

The same day I saw the Red-breasted, Apr. 27, 2005, I also watched a Pygmy, higher up near the top of Mount St. Helena. The bird flew over from Lake County and worked in the high pines. Very active and acrobatic, looked fluffy as it hammered in the bark, possibly in search of food. It was difficult to follow with my field glasses. They seem to be rare but breed regularly in Napa's forests. A fairly common bird in coastal areas of neighboring Sonoma County.

Creepers have striking wing patterns but even in flight they are not clearly visible, as they are so small and quick. Creep jerkily up tree trunks and large limbs, then fly down to base of next tree, creep up again, and so on.

● **Creepers** *Certhiidae* 1 sp. Mouse-like tree climber with thin, curved bill used to dig insects and larvae from bark. As with woodpeckers, stiff tail-feathers serve as a prop.

Brown Creeper
Certhia americana   fP

L 5¼" **Habitat**: Dense, shaded mixed forests of redwood, oak and fir, with large and dead trees; also in old-growth oak woodland. Nest is built behind loose bark or a narrow crevice in a tree.

Well-camoflaged against a tree trunk with their brown spotted plumage. Usually detected first by ear. Call is a very high thin 'scree' resembling the Golden-crowned Kinglet. The high-pitched variable song 'tsee see see teesswee see' is often heard. Generally solitary or in pairs but in winter joins feeding parties of small birds with chickadees, warblers and kinglets.

● **Wrens** *Troglodytidae* 6 sp. North America is wren country, with 9 species (Napa 6) while in all of Eurasia there is only one, the Winter Wren. Most are small, brown, active and secretive, and raise their tail. All have a loud song.

Winter Wren
Troglodytes troglodytes   uP

L 4" **Habitat**: Well-wooded moist western hills. In winter, also in Napa Valley and some canyons. Males build a number of nests within their territory to attract several females in different nests.

The smallest wren, brown with heavily barred flanks, its short tail is consistently cocked. A remarkably vigorous song, long and complex with a series of high tinkling trills, running on and on. Dwells principally in the undergrowth near streams in dense thickets and under fallen logs, like a small rodent.

House Wren
Troglodytes aedon   rW, cS

L 4¾" **Habitat**: From the remaining riparian woodlands in the Valley floor to densely wooded foothills, but tend to avoid residential areas unlike those in the eastern states.

Plainer, more gray-brown than most wrens. Has a faint 'eyebrow.' Long tail is less often raised than that of the smaller Winter Wren. Shy but curious, popping up in the open, disappearing again; hyperactive and not easy to observe. Song is a fast, bubbly series of musical notes, not as varied as the Bewick's or Winter Wren's; it reminded me of a European nightingale.

Marsh Wren
Cistothorus palustris   fP

L 5" **Habitat**: Common resident in the tidal marsh, but rare and perhaps no longer breeding at Wooden Valley. Males build several nests, some very close together, 1-3 ft. above water level.

Easy to identify in their unique habitat and also by color: dark crown with a prominent whitish 'eyebrow,' rufous on wing and dark striped mantle. Cocks its tail and shows the pale unbarred undertail coverts. Easy to observe from a boat but the birds are very shy when approached on land. Their loud song is a mechanical but musical 'pour tshee sheeet sheeet sheet.'

Canyon Wren
Catherpes mexicanus

uP

L 5¾" **Habitat**: Canyon walls and steep cliffs such as the Palisades and Mount St. Helena; also in boulder fields. Nest: an open cup on a ledge or in a crevice.

Chestnut-brown with a prominent white throat and breast and a very long bill. In Napa lives in the most remote and isolated places, and is not easy to observe. As indicated by its scientific name, translated from the Greek *Katherpein*, it 'creeps' like a rodent over the rocks and often quickly raises its tail, clearly distinguishing itself as a wren. Song: a cascading series of clear whistles.

Rock Wren
Salpinctes obsoletus

uP

L 6" **Habitat**: Rocky canyon sides, rocky fields and similar bad lands with rocks and boulders. Nest: a cup in a cavity, paved with small stones at the entrance.

A large, plain-looking wren with a long bill that lives between rocks and boulders on meager soil, often far from water. More often heard than seen, though it can be difficult to locate the bird from its soft Mockingbird call, 'tiou, tiou, ti oo,' repeated again and again. Does not raise its tail, but bobs up and down energetically.

Bewick's Wren
Thryomanes bewickii

cP

L 5¼" **Habitat**: Resident in bushy woodland, chaparral, drier thickets, gardens and bushes around houses. Nests in any cavity and accepts nest boxes.

This is the 'house' wren of Napa, found throughout the county from wilderness to suburb, as long as there is brushy cover. Plain in color, gray breast and most typically, the long white 'eyebrow' and long tail often flicked sideways. Longish and slender in appearance. Remains year-round in the county and is not shy. Its high-pitched, varied warbling song can be heard even on cold winter days.

● **Babblers** *Timaliidae* 1 sp. The only representative of this large, mostly Asian family of over 260 species lives exclusively along the Pacific, from Oregon to Mexico, in chaparral and brushland.

Wrentit
Chamaea fasciata

fP

L 6½" **Habitat**: Common in chaparral and similar dense brushland. Visits old overgrown gardens, usually in fall. Nest: a compact cup in a dense shrub.

Usually hard to see in their brushy habitat, but both sexes sing and their loud whistling song, like a ping-pong ball bouncing on a table, is often heard. Rarely on the ground, they keep to dense cover in search of insects generally taken from bark. In fall they also take small soft berries and in winter, seeds. Once established, they are extremely sedentary. Younger birds will move around to find new territories.

Not a wren, [image] or a titmouse. It has been placed in different families. Now, after new studies, it appears that the Wrentit is a babbler or an Old World Warbler.

Vineyards keep expanding and there is great need for conservation of the biodiversity in surrounding areas. Placing nest boxes has been widely promoted and very successful when done properly. (If you wish to know more see p. 13 for details.) Bluebirds are one of the species that has profited from this program.

● **Thrushes** *Turdidae* 7 sp. A large family. Some are familiar sights while others are shy forest dwellers. Generally they forage on the ground. Some thrushes are among the finest singers.

Western Bluebird fS
Sialia mexicana

L 7" **Habitat**: Oak savannah, fenced meadows, roadsides, vineyards, orchards. The presence of cavities in trees or posts, old woodpecker holes or nest boxes are very important.

A very familiar and much loved bird; usually seen in pairs, often along roadsides. In fall they gather in large flocks when searching for insects, their main food, and can literally cover a lawn in front of a house. Also eat small berries such as mistletoe. Females are variable in color, from mostly drab gray to more brownish, but their tail and flight feathers are always blue. The breast color also varies and, as the males, some have chestnut on their back.

Mountain Bluebird, *Sialia currucoides* An irregular visitor from the Sierra. Male all blue; the gray female has no orange on her breast but blue in wing and tail (see p. 111).

Hermit Thrush cW, uS
Catharus guttatus

L 6¾" **Habitat**: Breeds in shaded mountain forests, where the nest, hidden by plants, is built near or on the ground. In winter common in every kind of forest, chaparral and garden.

A very quiet and unobtrusive bird; spends most of its time in the undergrowth or on the forest floor. Often seen hopping on long legs on a mountain trail, where one can also find glossy blue shells from hatched eggs. The male has one of the most beautiful songs of all Napa birds.

Swainson's Thrush uS
Catharus ustulatus

L 7" **Habitat**: A rare summer visitor; breeds in the hills in wet thickets, and in dense willow forests along Valley streams. Nest is built in a low tree or bush.

Very similar to the Hermit Thrush with a more reddish-brown mantle but less red tail, and only faint spots on breast. Generally sings at dusk, a flute-like song, smooth and rolling with an abrupt end. Unlike the Hermits, their blue eggshells have small reddish speckles.

When young bluebirds leave their nest, they look quite different from their parents. The wings have grown to nearly full
size but the tail is much shorter. Their general color is smoky
gray with paler spots, but the flight feathers and tail are already blue. Birds do not replace their wings and tail until the
next spring, but the body changes in late summer so that 1st
fall birds resemble ads.

The juv.s of the two Catharus thrushes, Hermit and Swainson's,
are similar but the Hermit already has a more rust-colored
tail, and underparts are pale buff to white, heavily spotted
black. The Swainson's in general is darker, has pale lores,
the underparts are more gray-buff with fainter barrings and
spots. Both are heavily spotted with pale buff dots on their
head and, like the juv. bluebirds, also on their upper parts.
The Robin (also a thrush) is much bigger and the basic colors
are similar to the adult fem. with extensive pale spots above
(with dark tips) and black spots on breast and belly. The juv.
Varieds resemble their mother, with darker-tipped throat and
spotted breast band.

juv
Bluebird

Catharus
thrushes
leave their
nest when
10-12 days old

Robin

Varied Thrush

juv Robin
about 15 days old

Some female Robins resemble males and some males can have
the dull look of a female. Usually the females are paler with
less contrast in colors. After the breeding season, before they
molt, the colors of both sexes appear really worn out.

♀ worn
plumage

cW, fS   **American Robin**
          Turdus migratoris

L 10" **Habitat**: Only breeding in the
county since 1914. Common in gardens
and orchards, now also in shaded mixed
woodlands and canyons throughout
the county.

One of the most familiar birds. It is common
to see them hopping over a lawn in search of
earthworms. Robins have profited for food and
nesting and feeding in winter from all kinds of
human activities: irrigation of land and planting
of fruit trees and berry shrubs. Usually double-
brooded. In fall many more birds arrive from the
north and remain in Napa in winter.

♀

uW   **Varied Thrush** ▷
                      Ixoreus naevius   ♂

L 9½" A winter visitor but numbers vary greatly from year
to year. Quite possibly overlooked since they are elusive and
prefer dense shaded and damp woodlands, especially coniferous forests. Similar to a chunky smaller Robin with orange
eyebrow and distinctive wing pattern.

♀ similar with
grayer, paler,
pale breast band

87

Four families:
Thrashers and mockingbirds belong to the thrush-like family of **Mimids: *Mimidae***; 4 sp. well known for their song.
The **Waxwings: *Bombycillidae***; 2 sp. are a small northern-hemisphere family named after the waxy droplets on their secondaries.
The related **Silky Flycatchers: *Ptilogonatidae***; 1 sp. a New World family of long-tailed gregarious birds of which the black Phainopepla is the most northern representative.
Dipper: *Cinclidae*; 1sp., looks like a bold overgrown wren, with an unusually aquatic life in fast-flowing streams.

Their song is partly sweet and musical, partly harsh, choppy and guttural. The singers vary in excellence; some can be confused with a mockingbird, others lack brilliance

California Thrasher

juv

wing jerking

ad

Northern Mockingbird

Mockingbirds are very playful and territorial birds. Their black and white tail and wing patterns play an important part in their social behavior.

Northern Mockingbird   cP
Mimus polyglottos

L 10" **Habitat:** Common permanent resident in all urban, suburban and most rural agricultural areas; loves orchards. Absent in most of the upland regions of the north and northeast. First recorded as a breeding bird in Napa County in 1935.

In spring the male's life is singing and fighting. No other Mocker is allowed to enter his territory and his beautiful song can be heard day and night. Each male has his own song of varied phrases, repeating each several times. In fall the females might also sing a short song to establish a feeding territory. While their song is melodious, their call is a loud, harsh 'cheack.' Generally feeds on insects, but in fall and winter also on berries and fruit, and will defend a fruiting tree or shrub from any other bird.

fP   △
△

California Thrasher
Toxostoma redivivum

L 12" **Habitat:** Common in chaparral, less frequently in shrubby rural gardens adjacent to their natural habitat. Nests near the ground in low, dense shrubs, native or exotic. Has a long breeding season from Feb.-Sep.

Like the Mockingbird, the Thrasher is also a fine singer: a bit low with some scratchy notes, repeats each phrase once or twice but lacks the brilliance of the Mocker. Sings on a perch sticking out of cover, from which it can quickly retreat at the slightest danger. Their call is a dry 'cheack.' With its strong, long curved bill, long tail and rufous undertail coverts, this Thrasher is unmistakable. Usually seen on the ground pecking in soil, tossing leaves aside, never far from cover; always active and noisy.

In fall and winter their main diet is berries, native and exotic; a flock can strip a bush very quickly. Toward spring, insects become more important.

cW, exS ● **Cedar Waxwing**
Bombycilla cedrorum

L 7¼" **Habitat**: Regularly breeds in California in open coniferous or mixed forests along the northwest coast, exceptionally farther south. An occupied nest was found in Napa County in Jun. 1973 at Linda Falls. In winter sometimes gathers in large flocks, wherever fruit and berries are plentiful.

During Sep. compact flocks of waxwings arrive from the north. Depending on food availability, large numbers remain in Napa throughout the winter, or they may move as far south as Mexico. Their movements are very irregular. A Cedar Waxwing can be confused with a Bohemian (p. 116) and, in flight, also with a European Starling, which has a similar silhouette.

rPt ● **Phainopepla** ▷
Phainopepla nitens

L 7¾" **Habitat**: Dry mesquite brushland. Extremely rare in Napa; most likely to be found in dry, live oak chaparral. Breeds in southern California in early spring in the hotter areas and raises a second brood in the central foothills, when most likely to be seen in the county. Nest is sometimes placed in a mistletoe tangle well up a tree.

Phainopepla, which means 'shining dress,' is the name of this striking, glossy, elegant bird. Appears all-black at a distance but in flight the large white primary panel shows up clearly. The female is plain gray with some pale edges to wing feathers. Nomadic and irregular in their habits. After breeding, they wander around in search of mistletoe berries.

rW, LxS ● **American Dipper** ▷
Cinclus mexicanus

L 7½" **Habitat**: Cool, clear, rushing mountain streams with rich aquatic insect life; a rare habitat in the county and therefore distribution of the Dipper is limited to Rector and Milliken Canyons. Possibly only one pair breeds. Uses same nest site each year. Males could be polygamous.

An astonishing songbird; never found away from fast-flowing mountain waters; has adopted water as its element. All food is taken underwater, mostly larvae of mayfly and caddis fly. When they use their wings underwater, or walk on the stream bottom between rocks and boulders in search of food, it can look like it is flying. Has a loud, musical wren-like song.

Ruby   Golden ♂

Male Kinglets have a red crown patch like a crest, which is usually concealed. They are territorial during the breeding season, singing vigorously, raising their crest to impress any other Kinglet intruder. They also show their crest in courtship display, as illustrated above.

juv

ad ♀

— yellow feet like Golden

Ad. and juv. are very similar but the juvenile has no red on crown (concealed in ad..). Compare also Hutton's Vireo (p. 77) and *Empidonax* flycatchers (p. 74-75). The juv. Golden-crowned above has a striped face.

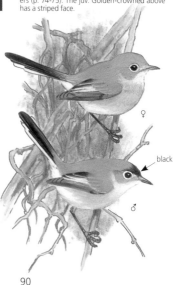

♀

black

♂

● **Kinglets:** *Regulidae* 2 sp. Small but compact, short-winged and short-tailed active warbler-like birds, with large eyes and needle-like bills for gleaning tiny insects from leaves and conifer needles.

Both the Golden- and Ruby-crowned spend most of their time foraging in trees and bushes, often in company of other small birds like the similar Hutton's Vireo (p. 77), chickadees or warblers. The Golden-crowned favors high conifers while the Ruby-crowned can come into gardens to search for insects in lower bushes. The Golden-crowned's call is a high and thin 'zee-zee-zee' and the Ruby-crowned's call is a much huskier 'ji-dit,' and their songs are different.

Golden-crowned Kinglet   uW
Regulus satrapa

L 4" **Habitat**: Uncommon winter visitor in spruce and other coniferous woodlands but also in broadleaf evergreen forests. There is no confirmed breeding record for Napa County.

I heard the song of this kinglet when walking down a trail from Mount St. Helena and watched a pair while the male was courting. I had seen this in neighboring Sonoma County, where they breed toward the coast and possibly along the border with Napa. They could also breed here. Perhaps they have been overlooked, since they are mostly high up in tall conifers, where their small size and thin calls make them difficult to detect.

Ruby-crowned Kinglet   cW
Regulus calendula

L 4¼" **Habitat**: A common or even abundant winter visitor, mostly seen in deciduous woods and thickets, gardens and parks. Breeds in California in sub-alpine coniferous forests; there is no breeding record in Napa County.

Hyperactive, moves restlessly from one bush to another, often in company but also alone, inspects every branch and leaf for its main food, tiny insects and their eggs. Its song is quite loud for such a small bird, varies greatly in different individuals and is extremely musical; usually heard toward spring before departure to breeding quarters.

● **Old World Warblers** *Sylviidae* 1sp. A large Old World family, with only four almost identical representatives in North America, of which the Blue-gray is the most widespread. Tiny birds with long tails.

Blue-gray Gnatcatcher   fS
Polioptila caerulea

L 4½" **Habitat**: Common in blue oak country and chaparral, and similar brushy woods. Breeds from Apr. to Jul.; territorial. Nest: a neat, deep compact cup saddling a tree branch.

With their small size and long tail, often cocked, the silhouette resembles a wren but their color is unique. Difficult to observe, on the move flitting from shrub to shrub, or high in leafy trees, gleaning insects and their eggs from the branches and leaf surfaces. They catch gnats, of course, but all kinds of insects as well, including spiders.

Warbler identification is not an easy task. Males, when in their bright breeding plumage from Mar.-Aug., pose no problems. It is the less bright females and especially males in fall dress or 1st winter plumage that are often so confusingly similar. Some resemble vireos in coloring (p. 77) but vireos have stronger bills. Since warblers are so active and always on the move, identification is even more difficult.

● **Wood Warblers** *Parulidae* 15 sp. A very large and successful family of over 115 species; all live in the Americas from Alaska to Argentina, 53 sp. occur in North America, of which most spend the winter in south of the U.S. Mainly insectivores, but during migration and winter, many take nectar and fruit.

Orange-crowned Warbler
Vermivora celata
rW, fS

L 5" **Habitat**: Common in chaparral, riparian tangles and brushy edges of mixed forests throughout the county. Their bulky nest is placed in shrubby growth on or near the ground.

Don't look for the orange crown, present but difficult to see. The most drab and uniformly colored warbler; some can appear yellowish green, others, like the passage migrants that breed in the interior western U.S., are often grayish, with yellow undertail coverts.

Nashville Warbler
Vermivora ruficapilla
rTS, xST

L 4¾" A bird of open woodland, often in second growth, that breeds in the high mountainous areas of California. A relatively rare spring and fall migrant; there is no Napa breeding record. Rather short-tailed, similar to the Orange-crowned, with a gray head and contrasting yellow underside. The rusty-orange crown patch is usually concealed or missing in the duller female. Both sexes have white eye rings.

♀ less yellow and duller

Yellow Warbler
Dendroica petechia
uS

L 5" **Habitat**: Common in willows and alders, along streams and ponds. Breeds May-Jul. The nest is a neat, compact cup fixed in a forked twig. Only the female incubates.

♀

♂

From Alaska to Peru, a most successful and widespread warbler, and the only warbler breeding in the Galapagos Islands. Usually unmistakable, the only all-yellow bird. Some individuals are drab in color and could be confused with an Orange-crowned Warbler, particularly the female, which can be very dull.

Yellow-rumped Warbler
Dendroica coronata
cW, LxS

L 5½" **Habitat**: Abundant in the lowlands in winter and during migration periods. Breeds in mixed pine, fir and oak forest in the northwest corner of Napa County.

"Audubon's"

♂

♂

nbr fall/winter

So common in winter, often seen in small flocks. Found very locally during the breeding season. In 2006 it was discovered that forests east of Mount St. Helena support about 25 breeding pairs. In their first winter dress, a rather drab brownish color, but the yellow rump is already present in both sexes.

"Audubon's Warbler" It is this yellow-throated form which very recently was discovered to breed in Napa County. Normally has a larger white wing patch but this is not a reliable fieldmark.

♀ more gray on head and duller

"Myrtle"

♂

"Myrtle Warbler" A more northern and eastern breeder, with a white throat, black ear coverts and a narrow white stripe above the eyes, which is typical for both sexes. In Napa, a passage migrant and winter resident.

fall imm;
ad have
chestnut flanks

white

black ♀

black ♂

black

♀

♂

♀

♂

♂ has
white throat

sexes similar

Chestnut-sided Warbler
Dendroica pensylvanica
xVa

L 5" **Habitat**: Breeds in the eastern side of North America and is a rare visitor to the Pacific states, usually in fall, sometimes in spring. Migrating birds can occur anywhere but prefer riparian habitats. In first fall plumage the chestnut flanks are absent, the back is unstreaked lime green but the yellow crown, a good field mark in all dresses, is present. Tail is often held raised.

Black-throated Gray Warbler
Dendroica nigrescens
fT, uS

L 5" **Habitat**: Higher elevation in the transition zone between live oak woodland, interspersed with knobcone pine, Douglas fir, juniper or manzanita and the conifer forests.

While the Napa summer residents are building their nests in limited habitat at higher elevations at the end of Apr., migrants are still passing in the foothills toward their northern breeding haunts in Canada. Unlikely to be confused with any other warbler, but see the Black-and-white below.

Townsend's Warbler
Dendroica townsendi
rW, uT

L 5" **Habitat**: Resembles a yellow version of the Black-throated Gray, which it replaces further north up to Alaska, where it breeds in coniferous forests; a common transmigrant in spring and fall. Some stay all winter in oak and riparian woodland or conifer forests. Often overlooked since they usually feed in tall evergreen trees during winter. Interbreeds with Hermits where their ranges meet.

Hermit Warbler
Dendroica occidentalis
lxS

L 5" **Habitat**: Extensive conifer forests. Normally breeds in cooler parts of California from mountains to near the coast. Only recently found as a breeder in the county.

Like a Townsend's with a yellow face and unstreaked flanks. In fall young females appear washed out and drab with no black on their throat. Hermit is not a well chosen name for this bird as it is often seen travelling in flocks with other warblers during migration. Some might remain here and be seen in mixed winter flocks.

Black-and-white Warbler
Mniotilta varia
xVa

L 5¼" A good name for this bird would have been Creeper or Nuthatch Warbler, since it searches for insects on tree trunks and large branches, often upsid-down like a nuthatch. Resembles the Black-throated Gray above but has a different face and wing pattern and much longer bill. Its most different characteristic is its creeper-like behavior. An eastern bird and rarely seen on the Pacific side.

Northern Parula
Parula americana
xTa

L 4½" Also an eastern bird and only a casual spring and fall migrant in California. There is a single spring record in Napa County but since they keep to the treetops in search of insects, they may be overlooked. Spring migrants might sing and are more easily noticed. The song is a rising buzz: 'zz'zz'zzzeeeeeee tzewp.' It ends abruptly.

MacGillivray's Warbler
uT, exS
Oporornis tolmiei

L 5¼" **Habitat**: Dense thickets in wet, shaded upland canyons. There is one recent breeding record. Regular passage migrant in riparian lowland in Aug.-Sep..

A shy bird, it favors dense, impenetrable cover and is difficult to observe. A rare spring migrant, late Apr.-May, when males occasionally sing and may be mistaken for territorial birds. A common summer resident north of Napa County; there are fewer than five nesting records here, the last at Van Ness Creek in 2004.

Common Yellowthroat
uW, fT, uS
Geothlypis trichas

L 5" **Habitat**: The inland ssp. *arizela* lives in wet riparian thickets and fresh-water marshes. The saltmarsh ssp. *sinuosa* is relatively common in tidal marsh, a limited habitat.

Two yellowthroat ssp. breed in Napa; the rare inland form with a narrow white forecrown band and the more common, dark saltmarsh birds, are separated only a few miles by different habitat preference, as are the Song Sparrows (p. 113). Males are easy to identify but females can be confused with other warblers (see p. 91).

Wilson's Warbler
fT, uS
Wilsonia pusilla

L 4¾" **Habitat**: Dense moist under-growth in mixed forests, and riparian woods with willow and alder thickets. Nest: on the ground, hidden in moss or tussock-grass.

Uncommon summer resident, the first males arrive in mid Apr., before the females, and establish their breeding territory. By end of Oct.. all have gone, most to Central America. Male and female are bright yellow on the underparts and the male has a typical black cap.

Yellow-breasted Chat
IrS
Icteria virens

L 7½" **Habitat**: The densest riparian growth along water courses, especially in thickets of willow and blackberry. Nest: from ground level up to 5 ft. in dense shrub or tangle.

A large, aberrant warbler with a stout bill and long rounded tail. The unique song, heard day and night, is remarkably varied and ongoing–hoots and whistles. Once common along the Napa River where it has almost disappeared as a br. Winters in Central America from Sep.-mid-Apr.

sexes similar

Northern Waterthrush
xVa
Seirus noveboracensis

L 6" A rare fall, passage migrant on the way to Central and South America, there is one fall record. Looks more like a pipit or a small thrush than a warbler. Usually found in wet or damp forest edges near slow-moving rivers or standing waters. Walks on the ground near water's edge or on logs, permanently wags its tail, turning over leaves and searching for food.

As with the warblers, identification of Sparrows, these little brownish, streaked birds, is not always easy. Their shape and head pattern are usually of more help than their color. Some are conspicuous but others remain hidden in vegetation, except in spring, when males sing from an open perch, announcing their territory and to attract a female.

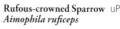

● **New World Sparrows** *Emberizidae* 24 sp. They are part of the large worldwide Bunting family of about 320 sp. Most are territorial during the breeding season, in which they eat mostly insects and feed their young on them exclusively. In fall and winter they form large mixed flocks, forage together and eat mostly seeds.

Rufous-crowned Sparrow uP
Aimophila ruficeps

L 6" **Habitat**: Arid chaparral with scattered small oaks, areas of open grass and rocky outcrops. The thick-walled nest is built on the ground at the base of a clump of grass.

I saw them once in Napa on a dry, steep, rocky hillside. While the grass in the Valley was still green, there between the rocks it was already golden. Not shy, several single birds were easy to observe from a distance. They appeared rather long-legged and long-tailed. Their call alerted me: a peculiar laughing 'dear-dear-dear.'

Chipping Sparrow xW, rS
Spizella passerina

L 5½" **Habitat**: Open country with scattered trees where light can penetrate to the ground, covered with short grass. Nests in shrubs or trees 3-20 ft. up, well-hidden in foliage.

A very neat, slim little sparrow with a distinctive rusty cap and white eyebrows; the larger Rufous-crowned has gray eyebrows and a pale malar stripe. In winter much duller, as drab as a female House Sparrow. Spends the winter mostly in Mexico and the first males arrive back in Napa Valley toward the end of Mar. Not common, they stay away from human habitation, unlike those in the eastern states.

Black-chinned Sparrow exS
Spizella atrogularis

A rare sporadic spring and summer resident in dry rocky chaparral. Prefers the low new growth in burnt areas, two years after fire. When growth becomes too high, the bird abandons the area. Quiet in its habits and might easily be overlooked. It has nested at least once in the county. Could be confused with a junco (p. 96) but back and wings are similar to other *Spizella* sp.

Lark Sparrow uP
Chondestes grammacus

L 6½" **Habitat**: Any dry open country with scattered trees and bushes, broken chaparral, blue oak woodland and foothill pines. Nest: on the ground, often in loose colonies.

Large stocky build with a striking head pattern, broad white sides and tips on their tail, distinctive when flying away; widespread throughout the county. Most common in the northeastern foothills in open blue oak woodland, absent from the marshes. Winter flocks seldom mix with other sparrows and stay near their breeding haunts.

ad br

ad nbr

♂ br
♀ and ♂ nbr similar; no black mask

sexes alike

The immature of these sparrows resemble their parents. The rusty or rufous colors are replaced by dull grayish-brown tones. The Black-chinneds look more like females, with no black mask and duller striped back.

Vesper Sparrow
Pooecetes gramineus

L 6¼" In the west, a bird of dry open ranch country. Seen only twice in the county, in Jamieson Canyon and Pope Valley. Should be looked for among other sparrows. Slimmer than the Lark Sp., with only a faint head pattern, a broad pale malar stripe, striped breast and flanks. Resembles a Savannah Sparrow but has white outer tail feathers.

Sage Sparrow
Amphispiza belli

uP

L 6" **Habitat:** Locally common but erratically distributed over the county, mostly in arid, open chaparral ridges and tableland.

black spot

During the breeding season, the territorial males sing from an exposed perch just above their dense domain; otherwise they would pass unnoticed. At the slightest danger, they drop down and disappear amongst the vegetation, where they spend their solitary lives all year. When perched, wags its long tail; holds it upright when running over open ground.

Savannah Sparrow
Passerculus sandwichensis

fW, rS

L 5½" **Habitat:** Open grassland, most common in the weedy grassland margins of the tidal marshes. Nest: on the ground in a hollow scrape concealed by overhanging vegetation.

One of the most common and widespread sparrows in North America, breeds from Alaska down to Mexcio and, oddly, is named scientifically after Sandwich Bay, Alaska. A migrant bird, but resident along the California Pacific coast. Generally prefers to stay out of sight in long grass, its preferred habitat. Similar to the rare Vesper and common Song Sp., but in flight no white is seen in the square tail and the Song Sparrow has a rounded tail.

Grasshopper Sparrow
Ammodramus savannarum

lxS

L 5" **Habitat:** Ungrazed fields along Partrick Road. Rare in the county. They like well-drained grassland where they build their nest in a small hollow, covered by overhanging grass.

We tried several times to find singing males along Partrick Road, listening for their buzzy insect-like song without success; several males were observed there in Apr. A peculiarly shaped sparrow with a big head, short tail and nondescript colors, except for a broad stripe above the eyes. Usually remain in their grassy covers and prefer to run instead of fly away when approached.

Lincoln's Sparrow
Melospiza lincolnii

uW

L 5¾" Like a smaller version of the variable Song Sparrow; breeds in boggy meadows on sub-alpine mountains up to 10,000 ft. In winter, inhabits moist lowlands with dense cover, where it is not easy to observe. Often solitary, which makes observation even more difficult, or in mixed flocks. In flight, like a Song Sparrow with a rounded but al-grayish tail. Flight call: a high buzzy 'szeet.' (Song Sparrow: a thinner 'seeet.')

nbr

M.m.gouldii

M.m.samuelis

juv.

♀

dark ♂;
some are
much paler

♂
♀ duller and
browner

ad. br.

1st w

Swamp Sparrow
Melospiza georgiana

xW, Ta

L 5¾" Widespread marshland sparrow common across North America east of the Rockies. They winter in the southeast states down to Texas and Mexico, and in a small strip along the U.S. Pacific coast; usually solitary and easily overlooked in their dense grassy habitats. Smaller than a Song Sparrow; rather dark overall with a gray face, rusty crown, and rufous wings and tail, which are visible in flight (gray in Lincoln's).

Song Sparrow
Melospiza melodia

fP

L 6¼" There are two different ssp. in Napa County: one in the tidal marshes ●, the other in moist thickets and beside streams, in the remainder of the county ● (see p. 113).

Common and widespread over North America; 39 ssp. are described, of which two are resident in Napa. Only the northern breeders migrate and occur in the county on fall migration or in winter. The forms vary greatly in size and color but their song, which is relatively complex with short notes and long trills, varies only slightly.

Fox Sparrow
Passerella iliaca

uW

L 7" Widespread over Alaska, northern Canada and the western U.S. Breeds in California but not in the eastern states. Eighteen ssp. are described, of which at least four occur in passage migrants or winter visitors in Napa; most common are the sooty-colored yellow-billed northwest coastal form or the gray-headed California mountain form. Typical of all is the rounded head, large-sized foxy-red-colored wings and tail. Usually seen in groundcover where they scratch in leaf litter for food.

Dark-eyed Junco
Junco hyemalis

cW, fS

L 6¼" **Habitat**: Breeds in mixed forrest and oak woodland, rare in the lowlands, common on hillsides in mixed oak land, and at higher elevations in moist conifer and oak madrone forests.

Oregon Junco, the local form that breeds in the county. Seen frequently in small groups on forest space dust roads, but also in woods that are not too dense, where they build their nest on the ground, typically beneath the cover of a fallen branch. In Napa they are permanent residents, becoming very common toward winter, when more arrive from cooler areas. Can form large loose flocks in the winter.

Slate-colored Junco breeds farther north up to Alaska and moves southwards in fall but most remain in the U.S. Rather variable in color and some females are similar in general appearance to Oregons. Their habits are the same. In winter when they mix in large flocks, it is difficult to distinguish them from the Oregons, which vary greatly in color.

Harris's Sparrow
Zonotrichia querula

xW, Ta

L 7½" This largest of all sparrows has a rather peculiar distribution. Breeds in open space spruce woods in the Canadian Northwest Territories and winters in the central states from Nebraska to Texas. Some stray west and have been observed on several occasions in the county. Unmistakable, even in drab 1st winter plumage with a mostly white belly and their large size.

White-crowned Sparrow
Zonatrichia leucophrys
cWT

L 7" The nearest breeding population is found along a narrow coastal strip in upper Sonoma County, where a resident yellow-billed race is very common. In fall birds with pinkish bills arrive in Napa County from further north for the winter, often in large flocks. Found in weedy areas, near woodland edges and agricultural land.

Golden-crowned Sparrow
Zonatrichia atricapilla
cWT

L 7¼" Also a common visitor in the county, arrives about mid-Sep. and the last might remain until mid-May. Larger than the White-crowned; the immatures are very similar in color. Adults are much darker with broad black 'eyebrows' that are white in the White-crowned. They often flock together in the same habitat in company with other sparrows or juncos.

White-throated Sparrow
Zonatrichia albicollis
rW

L 7" The smallest of the four *Zonatrichias*. Rather stockily built, with a rounded head and contrasting white throat in all plumages. Flocks together with others but prefers to remain close to shrubs and bushes for cover. Rare in the county, the first arrive about end Oct. and some stay until end Apr. Singly, they might visit bird feeders, often in company of White- or Golden-crowned Sparrows.

the white edges
show up well

juv

Spotted Towhee
Pipilo maculatus
cP

L 8½" **Habitat**: Any habitat with good cover and a thick layer of leaf litter, from lowland riparian thickets, mixed forests, shrublands and chaparral to gardens.

♀ similar;
duller,
grayish

Not shy, but usually stays in cover to forage on the ground, scratching noisily in loose leaf litter by kicking with both feet in search of hidden insects and seeds. More often heard than seen; a simple song, like buzzy trilling: 'che che che ZHeese' (here here here PLEase); call: a harsh whining 'zhreee' or 'chwaay.'

California Towhee
Pipilo crissalis
cP

L 9" **Habitat**: From dry chaparral to riparian thickets, open oak and pine woods and now very common in gardens and parks when there is brushy cover.

sunbathing

Not secretive in behavior, readily comes out in the open but never far from cover and easy to observe in most Napa gardens or at bird feeders. Highly territorial, the male proclaims his property with a metallic 'chink' and a sharply accelerated simple song with similar notes; remains in one area throughout the year.

Green-tailed Towhee
Pipilo chlorurus

xVS

ad

juv

L 7¼" A bird of dry mountain chaparral and open pine forests in northern and eastern California; winters in Mexico. In Napa only an accidental, passage migrant. On migration they favor dense, low cover near streams and might be overlooked. Smaller than other towhees but have similar habits and are easy to identify with their green upperparts and tail.

Chestnut-collared Longspur
Calcarius ornatus (also on p. 117)

xW

♂
nbr

long spur ⟶   ♀ similar

L 6" It is always worth looking closely at a flock of wintering sparrows or Horned Larks on a stubble field since other seed eaters, like vagrant longspurs, will mix with them. They are not easy to distinguish in their rather drab winter plumages. Chestnut-collareds have more white in their tail than larks. The similar Lapland Longspur (p. 117) has narrow white tail sides and some rufous in the wings.

The introduced House Sparrow is a member of the **Old World Sparrows**: *Passeridae* 1 sp. and not related to the New World Sparrows (p. 94) but gave them their name. **Pipits**: *Motacillidae* 1 sp. resemble small elegant thrushes and are part of a large Eurasian/African family. **Larks** *Alaudidae* 1 sp. an Afro-Eurasian family, of which the Horned Lark has the widest distribution.

House Sparrow
Passer domesticus

introduced, cP

♀

♂

L 6¼" A common, well-known non-native bird, often treated as a pest. Breeds successfully in towns, suburbs and ranches; due to reductions in livestock and changes in agriculture, their once enormous population is now decreasing. It is interesting to note that for unknown reasons they are becoming rarer and are disappearing from many towns in Britain and other European countries.

American Pipit
Anthus rubescens

cW

nbr
Aug-Mar

br Mar-Jul

L 6½" A high northern bird. Breeds in California only on alpine meadows in the highest Sierra Nevada. Winters in the county from end Sep. till late Mar.; mostly seen in small flocks on open fields and mudflats, where they are often very common. The size of a sparrow but much slimmer; often wags its tail when walking. Seldom seen perched on a branch. In flight the white outer tail feathers and high call 'psipp' are distinctive.

Pipit

Horned Lark
Eremophila alpestris

uP

juv Apr-Aug

♂

♀

L 7¼" **Habitat**: Treeless barren ground in the marshes, over-grazed pastures and the edges of the airport runway. Nest: on ground in a small hollow sheltered by a stone or plant tuft.

The little Horned Lark holds two records: it is the most widespread small bird worldwide and there are 46 ssp. described, of which at least 5 breed in California. Found throughout North America and Eurasia, with a small population in North Africa (only non-resident Barn and Bank Swallows have a similar but more southern distribution). Long-winged ground dwellers with a typical face pattern and in all plumage, the male appears to have little 'horns.'

● **Grosbeaks** *Cardinalidae* 5 sp. An entirely American family; stout, conical, often large-billed. They feed their brood with insects but eat mostly seeds and buds.

Rose-breasted Grosbeak
Pheucticus ludovicianus

xT

L 8" Replaces the Black-headed in the eastern U.S. and where they meet, will hybridize. Female and 1st winter males are not easy to separate from Black-headed, but look for their underwing colors in flight. Their habits, habitat preference, call and song are the same.

lemon yellow

buff yellow

1st W
Rose-breasted
similar

Black-headed ♀

Rose-breasted ♀

Black-headed Grosbeak
Pheucticus melanocephalus

fS

L 8¼" **Habitat**: Mature deciduous woods along streams, wooded canyons and mixed upland forests; gardens with good cover. Nest: in trees or shrubs in a forked twig 5-15 ft. up.

Males return from their Mexican winter quarters in the first week of Apr. and when they establish their new breeding territory, their rich melodious whistling can be heard, similar to a robin but faster. The valley is occupied first but they will breed everywhere except chaparral and oak savannah. Not shy, will visit backyard feeders when close to woodland. Easily identified by their typical colors, wing pattern and large bill.

Blue Grosbeak
Guiraca caerulea

xTS

L 6¾" A summer resident in the Central Valley and only a rare vagrant in Napa; most likely seen from Jun.-Oct. on open weedy fields with brushy patches and some damp ground. Unlikely to be confused with any other bird, except the smaller Indigo or a Lazuli female.

Lazuli Bunting
Passerina amoena

rS

L 5½" **Habitat**: Broken chaparral slopes with some trees for song posts, oak woodland edges, especially along streams. Nest: in low shrubby growth such as thistle patches or small trees.

It is such a colorful bird that it was chosen for the cover of ***Breeding Birds of Napa County*** (p. 11). In spite of their brilliant color, the bird is often overlooked, remaining mostly in cover. From end Apr. until early summer the male will often sing from an exposed perch or overhead wire, sometimes accompanied by his drabber/duller female. I watched a pair at the edge of a vineyard feeding in an abandoned meadow, and later the male sang from a willow tree.

◁ **Indigo Bunting**
Passerina cyancea

xTS

L 5½" The eastern counterpart of the Lazuli, and where their distribution overlaps, they will hybridize. A rare spring and fall migrant in California, there are only a few records for Napa County.

♀ Lazuli;
♀ Indigo
similar

♂ br

♂ nbr

br. ♂ looks black at a distance; nbr. ♂ is like nbr. Lazulis without white wing bars; ♀♀ of both sp. are nearly identical to each other.

1st fall

♀ variable in color depending on age and seasons. The Tricolored ♀ is darker, resembles the Bicolored ♀ and is often indistinguishable.

♂

● **Icterids** *Icteridae* 12 sp. Three different groups belong to this large, exclusively American family: the Blackbirds, Grackle and parasitic Cowbird; the Bobolink and Meadowlark; and the colorful Orioles (see p. 44-45). For technical reasons the Starling is placed between them.

Red-winged Blackbird cP
Agelaius phoeniceus

L 8¾" **Habitat**: Wet meadows, marshes, lakes, ponds, streams, roadside ditches; any habitat with water, from marshes to northeast hayfields and farm ponds.

The most abundant North American songbird and very common in the county. They take advantage of any manmade, newly created habitat and are often seen on a roadside beside a meadow, breeding in a roadside ditch when there is weedy or grassy vegetation; prefer to make their nest in cattails. Males defend a large territory and in ideal territories, males pair with several females.

Red-winged   **Bicolored**
phoeniceus   *mailliardorum*

"**Bicolored Blackbird**" In Central California's lowlands there lives a bird that is like a common Red-wing but is different in many ways. A similar population lives in Mexico, in the mountains between 3,000-7,500 ft. They have similar habits to the common Red-wings but their voice is different, and the males have no yellow stripe below the red epaulettes. I observed some around a small farm pond with some Tricolored males that were easy to separate, but not so the females. I could see no differences in the females present. It is possible they are a different species from the Red-winged Blackbird and not just a subspecies. Their scientific name would be *A. gubernator*, and for the California form *A.g. mailliardorum*.

♀

♂

Tricolored Blackbird rW, lfS
Agelaius tricolor

L 8¾" **Habitat**: Reedy freshwater marshes, ponds with dense vegetation, such as tules and cattails, or blackberry and overgrown weedy fields. Nest: in dense vegetation at ground level or several feet up.

A species of special interest in California. The first nest was found in Napa in 1986. Colonies of up to 100 pairs are recorded in the mid 1990s. In 2005 I was shown a colony at some small overgrown ponds surrounded by vineyards, where at least 300 males were courting, and later a small colony on a farm pond behind some buildings, overgrown with Himalayan blackberry, where a few males together with 'Bicoloreds' were singing and females were taking large larvae from floating vegetation on the water's surface.

Yellow-headed Blackbird LxS
Xanthocephalus xanthocephalus

L 9½" **Habitat**: Freshwater marsh with dense tule and cattail growth where it roosts and nests. The nest, a deep cup, is bound to several stems 2-3 ft. above water level.

Common in the Central Valley and Great Basin wetlands; rare and an irregular breeder in Napa, where the right habitat is limited. A colony nester, in Napa breeds with other blackbirds. The Marsh Wren (p. 84) might influence their breeding success. They puncture blackbird eggs because they compete for damsel flies as food. Yellow-heads will take most of their food with flocks of other blackbirds on grazed pastures or agricultural fields.

Bobolink xTa
Dolichonyx oryzivorus

L 7" Does not breed in California, it is generally an eastern bird and a great wanderer during fall migration on their way to southern Brazil, northern Argentina or the west coast of South America. There is one Napa County record in Sep. Darwin, the great British naturalist, even collected one on the Galapagos Islands. It is the most aberrant *Icterid.*, especially the female and nbr. male that resemble sparrows, with long wings and short spiky tails. Their flight call is a sweet 'pink'.

Bobolink

Western Meadowlark cP
Sturnella neglecta

L 9½" **Habitat**: Dry grassland, where it breeds and winters; less at edges of oak woodland and in hay fields. Breeding season begins mid-Feb. Nest: on the ground under overhanging grass.

Prior to settlement, the meadowlark's habitat was much different. Perennial grasses have been replaced by exotic annuals. No one knows how this has affected the number and distribution of meadowlarks. We are certain, however, that conversion of hayfields and pastures to other uses is shrinking their breeding range. At present, meadowlarks remain common, especially in winter. Their rich, gurgling song can be heard from any dry meadow. Their identification poses no problem when on the ground or on the wing.

101

Red-wings and Brewer's are often seen feeding together. The imm. and female Red-wings appear streaky with varying pale eyebrows.

Brewer's always seem uniform in color, never streaky, but patchy when molting into male plumage. The 1st basic plumage is less glossy.

cP

L 9" **Habitat**: Everywhere from town center to the last farm building in open country, with shrubs and trees for roosting and nesting.

Brewer's Blackbird
Euphagus cyanocephalus

No other bird has benefited so much from development of the landscape in towns, agriculture, ranching or along the highways; this blackbird is everywhere. The glossy male with white eyes and the female with drab gray-brown color and black eyes are easy to identify. Sedentary in the county and more arrive in fall from further north.

Great-tailed Grackle   xNb
Quiscalus mexicanus

L ♂ 18", ♀ 15" A generalist that can occur in any open area such as golf courses, with trees or shrubs nearby for roosting.

During recent years this grackle has undergone an explosive range expansion and in California is now found breeding in some coastal areas. There are records of only single birds in Napa. It has nested in Solano County, and is expected to do so in Napa.

Brewer's
1ˢᵗ basic plumage

♂

starling

juv

The juv., when independent from its host, will join flocks of cowbirds it has never seen before. They are slightly streaked and could be confused with a Red-wing ♀, but look for the conical bill.

♀

Wilson's
(p. 93)

juv.

In Napa the species most vulnerable to the parasitic cowbird are the Wilson's and Yellow Warbler, Hutton's and Cassin's Vireo, the Song Sparrow and even the Black-headed Grosbeak. Any warbler, sparrow or other small bird can be a victim.

Brown-headed Cowbird rW, uS
Molothrus ater

L 7½" **Habitat**: Forages in pastures, fields, savannah, open woodland, livestock corrals, farmyards, parks, gardens and everywhere small birds breed; only avoids forests.

It is possible that cowbirds were not present in Napa before European colonization. With development, they settled, increased rapidly and are now found all over the county; most often seen in small flocks or in company of other blackbirds. Slightly smaller than a Brewer's, have a bold appearance and brown head. The gray-brown female has a white throat and, as does the male, a stout bill.

The brood parasitism of the cowbird is well known. They used to follow large bison herds on the plains and developed a nomadic lifestyle with no time to rear their own brood. With cattle introduction, they are now found throughout the continent and are more sedentary. A female will lay up to 40 eggs in a season and the record is 77 eggs laid by one female. These are deposited in the nests of different species. Many eggs are ejected, or the nests are abandoned by the owner, so not every egg laid produces a youngster. Eggs only need 10 days incubation, so the chick hatches with an advantage over the host's chick. Sometimes several cowbird chicks are found in one nest. Only the strongest survive.

● **Starlings** *Sturnidae*
1 introduced species

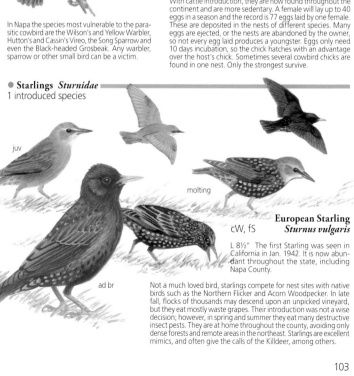

juv

molting

European Starling
cW, fS *Sturnus vulgaris*

L 8½" The first Starling was seen in California in Jan. 1942. It is now abundant throughout the state, including Napa County.

ad br

Not a much loved bird, starlings compete for nest sites with native birds such as the Northern Flicker and Acorn Woodpecker. In late fall, flocks of thousands may descend upon an unpicked vineyard, but they eat mostly waste grapes. Their introduction was not a wise decision; however, in spring and summer they eat many destructive insect pests. They are at home throughout the county, avoiding only dense forests and remote areas in the northeast. Starlings are excellent mimics, and often give the calls of the Killdeer, among others.

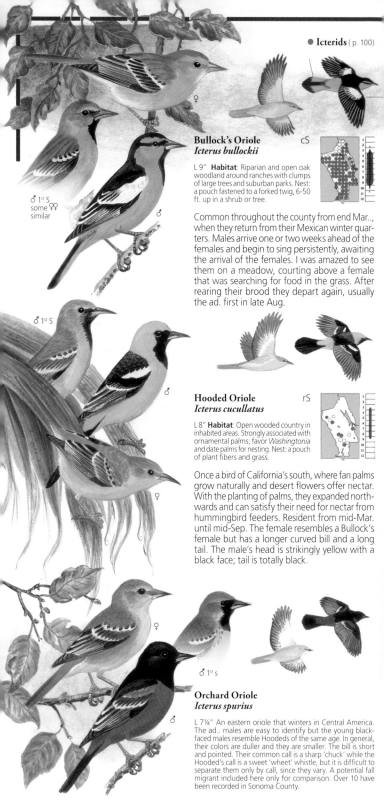

● Icterids (p. 100)

♀

Bullock's Oriole
Icterus bullockii
cS

L 9" **Habitat**: Riparian and open oak woodland around ranches with clumps of large trees and suburban parks. Nest: a pouch fastened to a forked twig, 6-50 ft. up in a shrub or tree.

♂ 1st S
some ♀♀
similar

♂

Common throughout the county from end Mar.., when they return from their Mexican winter quarters. Males arrive one or two weeks ahead of the females and begin to sing persistently, awaiting the arrival of the females. I was amazed to see them on a meadow, courting above a female that was searching for food in the grass. After rearing their brood they depart again, usually the ad. first in late Aug.

♂ 1st S

♂

Hooded Oriole
Icterus cucullatus
rS

L 8" **Habitat**: Open wooded country in inhabited areas. Strongly associated with ornamental palms; favor *Washingtonia* and date palms for nesting. Nest: a pouch of plant fibers and grass.

♀

Once a bird of California's south, where fan palms grow naturally and desert flowers offer nectar. With the planting of palms, they expanded northwards and can satisfy their need for nectar from hummingbird feeders. Resident from mid-Mar. until mid-Sep. The female resembles a Bullock's female but has a longer curved bill and a long tail. The male's head is strikingly yellow with a black face; tail is totally black.

♀

♂ 1st S

Orchard Oriole
Icterus spurius

♂

L 7¼" An eastern oriole that winters in Central America. The ad.. males are easy to identify but the young black-faced males resemble Hoodeds of the same age. In general, their colors are duller and they are smaller. The bill is short and pointed. Their common call is a sharp 'chuck' while the Hooded's call is a sweet 'wheet' whistle, but it is difficult to separate them only by call, since they vary. A potential fall migrant included here only for comparison. Over 10 have been recorded in Sonoma County.

A female oriole ejecting the egg of a cowbird that has just been laid in her nest, while the oriole male is fiercely chasing away the cowbird.

Oriole eggs

Cowbird eggs

Oriole eggs are long, oval and vary in their markings. Females recognize their own eggs. Cowbird eggs are more elliptical, finely spotted, a general egg pattern that resembles those of sparrows and warblers. Some birds will accept the cowbird egg, others abandon the nest and the oriole, which is strong enough, will eject it from her nest.

catching flying insect

bright ♀; some are much paler, grayer

br

♂ br

● **Tanagers** *Thraupidae* 1 sp. A large, very colorful, American family of mostly fruit-eating medium-sized birds. Only five occur regularly north of the Mexican border and they are largely insectivores during summer.

Western Tanager   rW, fT, uS
Piranga ludoviciana

L 7¼" **Habitat**: Common in the hills above the Valley in moist mixed forests with conifer stands. Found in remnant valley woodland at groves of wild plum.

A bright yellow-red-headed tanager singing its robin-like whistles from the top of a tall Douglas fir makes a beautiful picture. The call is a crisply rattled 'priterik,' and in flight, a softly whistled 'howee.' The female is rather drab, a bit like an overgrown goldfinch female. A summer resident from about Apr. until Oct. Small numbers overwinter.

♀

♂ 1ˢᵗ spring

♂

Summer Tanager
Piranga rubra

♂

L 7¾" No other bird in Napa can be confused with the all-red, large-billed male Summer Tanager. The female is dull yellow with darker olive-tinged back and wings. Breeds locally in southern California and is a casual visitor in the north. In surrounding counties there are a few records from almost every month of the year; Napa's single record is uncertain. Forages in the tree canopy, catching bees and wasps in swooping flights. Also feeds at lower levels in fruiting bushes and shrubs.

● **Finches** *Fringillidae* 9 sp. Seed-eaters with conical, sparrow-like bills. Males are brightly colored with red or yellow patches; females, drabber, like some sparrows. Undulating flight. Usually seen in flocks, constantly making contact calls.

◁ **Evening Grosbeak**   irW, ixTS
Coccothraustes vespertinus

L 8" Breeds in northern and eastern California in conifer forests at higher elevations, less often in mixed oak-conifer woods of northern lowlands. A sporadic winter visitor in Napa; numbers fluctuate from year to year. Sometimes seen in flocks in riparian woodland, feeding on box elder; also in rural gardens and parks.

House Finch   cP
Carpodacus mexicanus

L 6" **Habitat**: Originally, chaparral and riparian woodlands; now, for breeding and feeding, also abundant in urban gardens and parks, vineyards around ranches and farms.

Together with the Lesser Goldfinch, the most common and widespread smaller bird in the county; only absent from the higher elevations. This is the native bird that has taken most advantage of human settlement, not only in Napa but throughout the U.S. Their sweet, varied, warbling song can be heard from the center of the city of Napa to the last settlement in the north at Knoxville.

The intensity of the red in males varies greatly with individuals. Some are very bright. In others, due to their health and diet during the molting period and not related to their age, red is replaced by pale orange or even yellow.

Purple Finch   uP
Carpodacus purpureus

L 6" **Habitat**: Upland mixed forests and canyons with Douglas fir. Rare in the Valley's riparian corridor. Often with House Finches at feeders in urban areas in winter.

Stockier and shorter-tailed than a House Finch. Males have a deep raspberry hue, except for paler unstreaked flanks. Females have a faint face pattern and short dark streaks on the underparts. Their song is a rich, mellow, musical, ongoing warbling, which I heard often, but it was not easy to see the singer before it flew away; much easier to observe in winter flocks.

Cassin's Finch *Carpodacus cassinii*   xTa
L 6¼" A casual visitor. Paler than a House or Purple Finch with a bright red crown and long pointed wings. Females are easily overlooked and paler than a Purple female (see p. 111).

Red Crossbill   irW, ixSnb
Loxia curvirostra

L 6¼" The number of crossbills in the county fluctuates between winters. None have been seen for several years. Small flocks or single birds were usually found in the Angwin area at natural or ornamental conifers. Flocks in flight are noisy, calling a staccato piping 'gyp, gyp, gyp.' Nesting in the county is a remote possibility.

Pine Siskin
Carduelis pinus

fW, xST

L 5" **Habitat**: In winter, any open country wherever alder and ornamental conifers grow. Nest: high up in conifers, out on a branch, well hidden.

Siskin numbers have always varied in the county; winters with flocks of hundreds have been followed by years when none are seen. The first occur in fall, more and more arrive in winter, often in large numbers, but by mid-Apr. suddenly most have gone. There is one nesting record in the county.

sexes very similar

♂ Oct-Mar

♂ br

♀

American Goldfinch
Carduelis tristis

P

L 5" **Habitat**: Open country with weedy, overgrown fields, roadsides with thistles, chicory or flowers with some trees or shrubs for resting and nesting. Nest: a neat, nicely woven cup.

♀

♂ Mar-Oct

In winter, when goldfinches visit feeding stations, they may all appear to be females, but look at their shoulders: the male's are buffish yellow. In Mar.,they molt into bright yellow breeding dress. Seen most often in flocks feeding on thistle or other composites or resting together in a bush, sweetly singing their twittering song.

Lesser Goldfinch
Carduelis psaltria

cP

L 4½" **Habitat**: Almost everywhere, from suburban gardens and roadsides to open oak savannah. Usually in solitary pairs, breeds throughout the county. Nest: well-hidden in foliage, 5-10 ft. up a tree.

♂   ♀

♂

I believe this is the most common little bird in the county and I saw them every day. In Apr. flocks can still be common at niger seed feeders, while other pairs in the county will already be building nests. Males vary greatly in color, some have nearly black backs, and females are similarly recognizable in their individual colors.

Lawrence's Goldfinch
Carduelis lawrencei

xW, LS

♂

L 4¾" **Habitat**: Dry, open oak grassland, chaparral and similar dry country, often near a stream with weedy fields. Pairs nest singly, or in loose colonies.

♀

♂

Erratic and localized in its distribution. Napa lies just outside their main breeding range. There may be no more than 50 pairs breeding in the county. Feed on composite seeds like other goldfinches; especially fond of half-ripe fiddleneck seeds still in milk, which they feed to their nestlings.

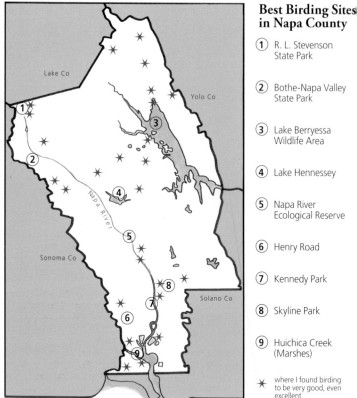

Best Birding Sites in Napa County

1. R. L. Stevenson State Park

2. Bothe-Napa Valley State Park

3. Lake Berryessa Wildlife Area

4. Lake Hennessey

5. Napa River Ecological Reserve

6. Henry Road

7. Kennedy Park

8. Skyline Park

9. Huichica Creek (Marshes)

✳ where I found birding to be very good, even excellent

Birding can be done anywhere. Within the city of Napa, House Finches breed in the vines creeping up buildings. House Sparrows are everywhere, and I even saw a Peregrine Falcon flying over the city. One will see many woodland birds that have adapted to town life. I heard Wild Turkey gobbling, and one early morning saw a flock walking across a private lawn and heard Mourning Doves and California Quail calling. I also observed Lesser Gold-finches, Oak Titmice, towhees, Bewick's Wrens and so many others, and they were never shy. Warblers and robins were next to juncos at the Tulocay Cemetery, a wonderful place for quiet birding. On the State Hospital's well-fenced grounds there is a large heronry with egrets and Night Herons. One can observe the birds from the road as they fly in and out. Enjoy the birds, but beware of the traffic. Often, observation of our fine feathered friends can be better from a distance.

Some places are certainly better than others to watch birds, and there are good days and poor days. Not only wind and weather influence the birds. On some days one just sees more than on other days, no matter how hard one tries. Often it is better to observe a single species closely rather than moving from one area to another. The best places are briefly described here. See page 109 for the title of a good little book.

1. Robert Louis Stevenson State Park:
   The most difficult and tiring, but one of the most fascinating places for birding. One has to climb a very steep trail to a more relaxing dirt road leading to the highest elevation in Napa County. This is described on page 110. The parking area is easy to reach from Highway 29.

2. Bothe-Napa Valley State Park:
   Best place for Pileated and five other woodpeckers, and the queen of all, the Spotted Owl. Most of the time one walks in the shade of beautiful second-growth forest, which is less tiring but more difficult from which to spot the birds. Best season: during breeding, from Apr. through Jul.

3. **Lake Berryessa Wildlife Area:**
Very accessible, even for the handicapped. Driving around the lake, every corner gives a new view and different birds. It is the best place to observe the two larger grebes, ospreys with nests, Bald Eagles and many ducks. At the north end of the lake, on the road to Knoxville, without leaving the car one may see wintering Lewis's Woodpeckers and resident Yellow-billed Magpies in the oaks and many passerine species in the meadows. Beware of other cars on the road. Best seasons: winter and spring.

4. **Lake Hennessey:**
Surrounded by a wide variety of habitats and good for all-round birding. Best for wintering waterbirds, loons, grebes, Tundra Swan, mergansers and different duck species. Osprey and the Bald Eagle breed here. A mixed rookery of Blue Herons and cormorants can be viewed from the road. The different woodlands around the lake are good for warblers and many other small birds. Also found: Northern Pygmy Owl and woodpeckers. Best seasons: fall, winter, spring.

5. **Napa River Ecological Reserve:**
A jewel surrounded by vineyards. Only 73 acres of riparian forest with picturesque growing valley oaks and meadows. Over 140 bird species have been observed in this reserve. Best for small passerines and a very good place to listen to birds singing, with the running water as background music. Keep to the trails as poison oak is abundant in this reserve. Best seasons: spring and fall.

6. **Henry Road:**
Pastures and vineyards form the landscape in the well-known Carneros District. Nearly 130 bird species have been observed, from Snow Goose in winter to Western Kingbird in summer. Best season is all year, and when there are no birds, there is good wine.

7. **Kennedy Park:**
Near Napa Valley College and the Municipal Golf Course. A good place for all wetland species as well as raptors. Red-shouldered Hawks breed, and Ferruginous as well as Rough-leggeds have been observed in fall and winter. The open flood plains across Napa River are great for abundant waterfowl and regular appearances of Peregrine Falcons. Best season: year round.

8. **Skyline Park:**
It is especially good for those interested in botany or good hiking. Best for all small passerines. Pied-billed Grebes, coots and Wild Turkey, passing by like domestic fowl, are easy to observe. Golden Eagles soar over the ridge and flocks of Band-tailed Pigeons pass by. There is an entrance fee, but well worth it. The birds are very used to visitors. Best season: year round.

9. **Huichica Creek:**
The most diverse habitats in a relatively small area. Tidal marshes, sloughs, grasslands, salt marshes and fresh, brackish and hypersaline ponds. All wetland birds are found here, too many to name, including ducks, waders, plovers, herons, egrets and the limited Samuel's Song Sparrow. (See p. 112-113 for more details.)

More about these fascinating places can be learned from the website of the Napa-Solano Audubon Society:
www.napasolanoaudubon.com

BEST BIRDING
IN NAPA AND SOLANO COUNTIES

Best Birding in Napa and Solano Counties
A site guide from the Napa-Solano Audubon Society written by local birders. May be difficult to obtain.

Mount St. Helena
and Robert Louis Stevenson State Park

The northern end of the long Napa Valley is dominated by 4,343 ft. Mount St. Helena. The peak lies
just a few yards outside Napa County but is best
accessed from this side. Take Highway 29 north
from Calistoga, up a winding road to undeveloped
Stevenson State Park, where parking is available on
either side of the highway. From here it is a five-mile,
tiring, steep trail in the shade of tall trees to the peak.
The climb is easier on reaching a dusty road. Mark
the exit of the trail or it may be difficult to find on
return. The views from the top are splendid, over
Napa Valley down to San Pablo Bay and across the
surrounding counties.

In Apr. 2005, not far from the peak, I observed a
Townsend's Solitaire and two Red-breasted Nuthatches
on the dead lower branches of tall conifers. White-
throated Swifts were flying up from Sonoma and
arching around the peak. I failed to see the Purple
Martins that breed up there. I was shown where Nut-
crackers had been observed in the Golden Chikapin
bushes. Mountain Quail were calling but not seen.
On our walk back, birding was great. There were
Peregrine and later Prairie Falcons just overhead, and
a Hermit Thrush in the shade of trees hopping along
the trail. Most exciting was a pair of Golden-crowned
Kinglets courting in the canopy of a tall Douglas fir,
which was on a steep slope and just at eye level
from my observation point. Amazingly there was
a Winter Wren near the parking lot singing loudly
as though holding a territory. The park is named in
honor of Robert Louis Stevenson.

A short list of some specialties and birds most
likely to be observed in this area:

br. = breeding birds
v = visitors

Kestrel	br.
Peregrine Falcon	v
Prairie Falcon	v
Mountain Quail	br.
California Quail	br.
Band-tailed Pigeon	br.
Western Screech Owl	br.
Great Horned Owl	br.
Northern Pygmy Owl	br.
Spotted Owl	?
Common Poorwill	br.
White-throated Swift	v ?
Vaux's Swift	v
Anna's Hummingbird	br.
Acorn Woodpecker	br.
Hairy Woodpecker	br.
Nuttall's Woodpecker	br.
Northern Flicker	br.
Pileated Woodpecker	br.
Olive-sided Flycatcher	br.
Dusky Flycatcher	br.
Cassin's Vireo	br.
Clark's Nutcracker	v
Pinyon Jay	v
Purple Martin	br.
Red-breasted Nuthatch	br.
Rock Wren	br.
Canyon Wren	br.
Bewick's Wren	br.
Winter Wren	br. ?
Hermit Thrush	br.
Townsend's Solitaire	v
Mountain Bluebird	v
Yellow-rumped Warbler	br.
Black-throated Gray Warbler	br.
Purple Finch	br.
Cassin's Finch	v

sexes alike

sexes alike

sexes alike

♀

♂

Clark's Nutcracker
Nucifraga columbiana

xTa

L 12″ A rare visitor from the high Sierra, where they
live and breed near the timberline in mixed coniferous
forests. Can occur regularly on Mount St. Helena when
the Golden chinkapin nuts are ripe, which, together with
pine seeds, are one of their favorite foods. Not shy like
many mountain birds and can easily be overlooked as
they search for nuts in bushes, but they constantly an-
nounce their presence with hoarse characteristic cries
such as 'Kra-aaaaa.' Easy to identify, nearly the size of a
crow with silver-gray plumage, black-and-white wings
and tail; most clearly seen in flight when crossing an
open space in a leisurely crow-like flight.

Pinyon Jay
Gymnorhinus cyanocephalus

X?

L 10½″ Lives on the eastern slopes of the Sierra in pine
and juniper forest. There are some doubtful Napa County
records. Most likely to be seen on Mount St. Helena but
could occur on any other high elevation in pine woods. In
some light can look a drab, dusky grayish-blue without
any contrast except for a deeper-colored head. Their call,
a nasal 'hoia hoia oiah,' is quite soft for a jay.

Townsend's Solitaire
Myadestes townsendi

luW

L 8½″ Common in the open juniper woods and conifer
forest edges in California's high mountains, where most
are resident. Birds breeding farther north in Canada are
highly migratory and in fall move south to Mexico's
mountains. Some arrive annually in Napa. As their name
indicates, solitary. Often seen perched upright in a tree
on a bare twig, swooping from it to catch insects in a
flycatcher's manner. A long slender bird, gray overall
with a typical wing pattern. A rather small head, rounded
belly and long tail. In flight the white sides on tail and
the buff wing stripes are good field marks. Their song
is a long warble, resembling a finch, which I heard at
the top of Mount St. Helena.

Mountain Bluebird
Sialia currucoides

xW

L 7¼″ Lives in similar open country to the Western
Bluebird (p. 86) but higher in the mountains. In winter
they often circulate in large flocks and can occur in lower
country away from their breeding haunts. A very neat,
tidy bird; the female is all gray with some blue in wing
and tail, and the male is all pale blue. Their wings are long
and pointed and the general impression is of a longer,
more slender bird than the Western Bluebird.

Cassin's Finch
Carpodacus cassinii

xTa

L 6¼″ Also a Sierra bird of high elevations, where they
live in dry pine forests. Rarely wander far from their
breeding haunts; just move lower down in winter. A
casual fall and winter visitor. Similar to the Purple Finch
(p. 106) with longer wings and tail, a straight more
pointed bill and paler color, more rose-red in the male
with a bright red crown. The female has a sparsely
streaked off-white breast and belly. Flight call: a dry
'tee-dee-yip' or 'chi-di-lip.'

111

The Marshes

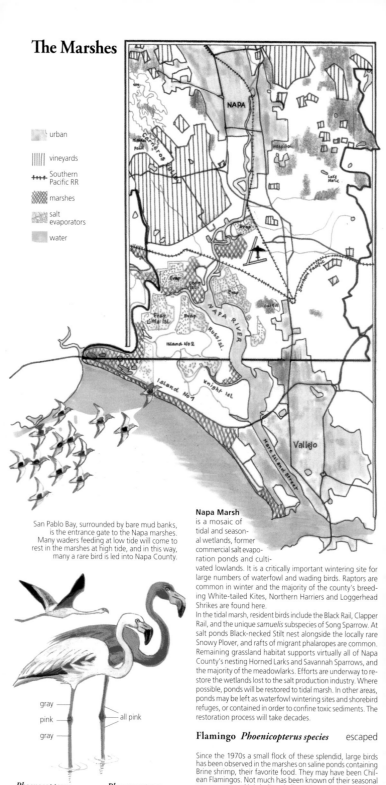

urban

|||||| vineyards

+++++ Southern Pacific RR

marshes

salt evaporators

water

San Pablo Bay, surrounded by bare mud banks, is the entrance gate to the Napa marshes. Many waders feeding at low tide will come to rest in the marshes at high tide, and in this way, many a rare bird is led into Napa County.

gray

pink

gray

all pink

Phoenocopterus chilensis

Phoenocopterus ruber

Napa Marsh

is a mosaic of tidal and seasonal wetlands, former commercial salt evaporation ponds and cultivated lowlands. It is a critically important wintering site for large numbers of waterfowl and wading birds. Raptors are common in winter and the majority of the county's breeding White-tailed Kites, Northern Harriers and Loggerhead Shrikes are found here.

In the tidal marsh, resident birds include the Black Rail, Clapper Rail, and the unique *samuelis* subspecies of Song Sparrow. At salt ponds Black-necked Stilt nest alongside the locally rare Snowy Plover, and rafts of migrant phalaropes are common. Remaining grassland habitat supports virtually all of Napa County's nesting Horned Larks and Savannah Sparrows, and the majority of the meadowlarks. Efforts are underway to restore the wetlands lost to the salt production industry. Where possible, ponds will be restored to tidal marsh. In other areas, ponds may be left as waterfowl wintering sites and shorebird refuges, or contained in order to confine toxic sediments. The restoration process will take decades.

Flamingo *Phoenicopterus species*   escaped

Since the 1970s a small flock of these splendid, large birds has been observed in the marshes on saline ponds containing Brine shrimp, their favorite food. They may have been Chilean Flamingos. Not much has been known of their seasonal movements and it is believed all may have died.

Song Sparrow subspecies

Birding in the Napa marshes generally means watching waders, ducks and the other waterside birds, but there is one special bird to look for. This is the Song Sparrow, *Melospiza melodia* (see also p. 96), which breeds across most of North America and varies greatly in size and color from region to region. Over 35 subspecies have been described, more than for any other bird. Usually they intergrade over a wide area from one population to another. This happens more frequently in California with its great variation in habitat. Fourteen subspecies are known to breed in the state, and three of them exclusively in a narrow coastal strip around San Francisco Bay. They are not in contact with each other and are permanent residents that do not leave their habitat. One of these subspecies, *M.m.samuelis*, is found only around San Pablo Bay in the tidal sloughs of *Salicornia* marshes in Napa, Solano, Sonoma, Marin and Contra Costa Counties. The second Napa subspecies, *M.m.gouldii*, is a freshwater, interior breeder usually found in the moist thickets beside streams in the Napa Valley.

"Marin" Song Sparrow *M.m.gouldii* This Song Sparrow is very common in freshwater vegetation south of the city of Napa, and in the valleys throughout the county. They are rare or missing from the moist canyons and springs in the foothills on the eastern side of Napa County. This bird and the following subspecies often live very close to each other in the marshes, separated only by their preference of habitat. It is not known if they interbreed.

"Samuel's" Song Sparrow *M.m.samuelis*. This subspecies makes its home in the tidal sloughs of the marshes. The birds are resident and territorial all year round and never go far from where they are born. They like to build their nests in the taller dense grindelia bushes, and search for food on the mud banks, and sometimes on floating vegetation but never far from cover. They avoid flying over wide open spaces because of their short wings. During high tides, they usually hide in the taller bushes and the male announces his territory from an exposed song post. The bird is very vulnerable in this isolated and limited habitat, and any further destruction or changes of habitat should be avoided. It would not only be a pity but a great loss if this unique bird should disappear from Napa County. It is a bird of special concern in California. The 14 California Song Sparrow subspecies remind me in many ways of the Darwin finches in the Galapagos Islands.

M.m.gouldii. Larger, with a longer tail than *samuelis*, they are paler in color, especially on the rump. The wings are a stronger chestnut brown. Their flanks have more brown streaks and some have a deeper gray-brown back.

M.m.samuelis. Smaller and much darker, more earth brown than the rufous-colored *gouldii* Their wings and rump are very dark, and underparts are off-white with dark spots rather than streaks. The beak seems to be smaller, but this varies and I saw one very dark bird with a really large, long beak. This appears to be a small and very dark-colored bird.

Rough sketches from my notebook, drawn while sitting in a rocking canoe. It may have been the best way to observe this bird as it was not shy, but not the best way to sketch! Later, while walking along its habitat, the bird was shyer and remained at a distance.

Rare Vagrants To complete the list of all birds recorded in Napa County, the rarest, perhaps seen only once or twice, are included on the following pages. However, some rare birds are covered in the main part of the book for easier comparison. Any migrating American bird can occur in the county in the future. While it is very unlikely that a sedentary Sage Grouse can be seen in the marshes, a non-migratory Blue Grouse is a possibility since it breeds in a neighboring county and perhaps once did in Napa. Birds like the Ibis may become a breeding bird as the restoration of the marshes progresses; at present it's just a dream. The Cattle Egret is more likely to breed. Any bird kept in captivity can escape and be seen in nature. The Mandarin duck (p. 28) is such a bird, which I include with the Wood Duck for comparison. On May 3, 2005, I heard a screaming *Aratinga* parakeet in the city of Napa. Had this bird escaped or was it from the San Francisco feral stock? When sighting a bird you believe could be a rare vagrant, contact a local ornithologist to verify your observation. One of the many good field guides of American birds can also help.

Western Gull
(p. 58)

Laysan Albatross *Phoebastria immutabilis*   xV
L 35" An aerial master of the open ocean, with a wingspan of almost 7 ft. Rarely seen from shore. After a Pacific storm in February 1994, this huge pelagic seabird found itself touring Sonoma and Napa Counties before hitting a powerline near Martinez. It was rescued, rehabilitated and returned to the sea. On occasion an albatross will enter San Francisco Bay aboard ship and require human assistance to get back to the Pacific.

juv

nbr
Aug-Jan

Brown Pelican *Pelecanus occidentalis*   IxS
L 51" A common summer and fall visitor along the nearby Pacific coast. A true seabird, seldom seen inland but there are Napa records. Smaller than the huge American White (p. 21), which appears even larger with its all-white plumage. Flies the same way, on flapping wings or relaxed gliding. The Brown Pelican's plunge diving technique for fishing is quite different from the White's. They are unmistakable in their gray-brown or silvery colors.

br

nbr Aug-Feb

Cattle Egret *Bubulcus ibis*   xW
L 20" A newcomer to the Americas; it first bred in South America in the 1930s after crossing from Africa, over more than 2,000 miles of open water. Initially bred in Florida in 1953 and spread rapidly across the U.S. to Canada. Some now breed in San Francisco Bay, and with the growing Snowy and Night Heron colonies will probably also breed in Napa one day. They need open fields and pastures, not necessarily near water, but livestock like cattle and horses are important so they can catch insects stirred up by their movements. More stockily built and shorter-legged than the Snowy (p. 22-23) but most distinctive is the yellow bill, similar to the much larger Great Egret. In br. plumage, bright yellow-orange crest, breast and mantle, and for a short while, red legs.

nbr
Sep-Feb

White-faced Ibis *Plegadis chihi*   xW
L 23" A few birds, sometimes together, have been observed in the marshes and on sewer ponds. Resemble an all-black curlew with a shorter but stronger bill. Like them they fly with neck extended, not retracted like herons. Ibis in California breed further inland. They nest in colonies, usually with herons, on low bushes or in tall reeds, but the Napa heron colonies are all in larger trees. If this ever changes, ibises could join a colony that is close to water. It's most unlikely they will start a colony themselves.

♀

♂ br

White-winged Scoter *Melanitta fusca*   xTa
L 21" In winter purely a sea duck on the Pacific coast. Might occur in the Napa marsh, but the single county record is from Lake Hennessey. All-black with a large 'nose' and a rather long, pointed tail. Best identified by large white 'panels' in black wings, often visible when flapping wings on water.

California Condor
Gymnogyps californianus
extirpated

L 46" ws 109" An egg of this magnificent bird was taken from a nest in Napa County in 1845 and is now in a museum in Russia. It's most unlikely that this huge scavenger will soar over Napa's vineyards. It could nest in the Palisades but there is not much game or livestock left to provide the carrion it needs.

Sandhill Crane *Grus canadensis*
xTa

L 45" ws 75" Blue Herons are often mistaken for cranes. Herons have longer bills and a different shape. Herons fly with retracted necks, cranes' are fully stretched. Also typical is the rooster-like bustle of feathers over the rump. There are two county records, both in the fall.

Solitary Sandpiper *Tringa solitaria*
xVs

L 8½" As its name suggests, often seen alone. Could occur anywhere wet, even small ponds or ditches. Resembles a dark, shorted-legged miniature Yellowlegs (see p. 52). Its clear flight call is 'peet-WEEt,' and dark underwings are typical.

Semipalmated Sandpiper *Calidris pusila*
xTa

L 6¼" Similar to Western Sandpiper (p. 54). An extremely rare fall migrant, favoring freshwater habitats. Semipalmateds have shorter bills and on average are darker, with plainer gray cap and back. More slender than the Western, and larger than the similar yellow-legged Least Sandpiper.

♂ nbr

variable

♂ br

nbr. ♂ similar but larger

♀

Ruff *Philomachus pugnax*
xTa

L ♂11½" ♀9" A Eurasian species. Unlikely to be seen in their picturesque breeding plumage, when every male has differently colored dress; white, rufous, black, barred or unicolored ruffs with differently colored crests. In winter the male is similar to the female but much taller. The female ruff in particular resembles a Pectoral Sandpiper (p. 55).

Parasitic Jaeger *Stercorarius parasiticus*
xW

L 16½" A coastal migrant, coming inland only during fall migration. Some might over-fly the county unnoticed. More elegant than a gull and heavier than a tern. Dark brown in all plumages, with a light wing panel.

Franklin's Gull *Larus pipixcan*
xW

L 14½" Larger than Bonaparte's (p. 60). Darker on back and short black bill. In br. plumage all-black hood; in nbr. a dark cap. Large white spots on wingtips. Longish dark legs. Juv. darkish brown above, with a black cap like ad. nbr.

nbr Aug-Mar

Little Gull *Larus minutus*
xV

L 11" An Old World species of which only a few breed in the Great Lakes region; a straggler on the West Coast. Tiny, behaves like a tern. Black hooded in br. plumage. Best field mark is the dark underwings.

nbr Aug-Apr

Common tern *Sterna hirundo*
xTa

L 12" Very much like a Forster's Tern (p.61). Only an expert can tell the difference. Primaries are more dusky, tail shorter, in nbr. plumage, dark carpal bar. In flight their wings seem darker with broad dusky tips on primaries.

nbr

Elegant Tern *Sterna elegans*
xTa

L 17" Similar but smaller than the Caspian Tern (p. 61). More elegant with a long, slender orange bill. In all plumages paler and the black cap ends in a fluffier crest. An uncommon bird in the San Pablo Bay area.

nbr Aug-Feb

very young birds have gray bills

ad

short-billed

long wingtips

short tail

short wingtips

long tail

relatively long bill, two-colored with dark tip

♂

♀

Rare Perching Birds: All the Passerines and one cuckoo are grouped together here. Most are insectivores and therefore migrants, and could occur in the county on their way to and from winter quarters farther south. Since they are small and don't sing during passage, many are overlooked, especially in the quick spring migration.

Yellow-billed Cuckoo   extirpated
Coccyzus americanus

L 12" The last nest of this cuckoo in the county was found in 1902. Their breeding habitat, old-growth riparian forest, has been destroyed. Only a few of the subsp. *C.a. occidentalis* breed in California and are listed by the State Dept. of Fish and Game as an endangered species. Some could still pass as rare vagrants but would not stay for long. As they like to keep in cover, they would usually be overlooked. In their breeding territory, they are rather noisy but not on migration. The subsp. of the eastern U.S. is a common bird.

Hammond's Flycatcher   xTS
Empidonax hammondii

L 5½" Very difficult to identify and the Hammond's prefers to perch high in trees to make it even harder. The bill is rather short, wingtips long and the well-notched tail short. Belly, a pale yellow, with an olive gray 'vest' on the breast. Clearly distinguished from other *Empidonax* (p. 74-75) by voice, but like most vagrants, rarely sings on passage. Song is a series of sharp, rough notes: 'tsi-pik,' a rough 'grr-vik.'

Gray Flycatcher   xTS
Empidonax wrightii

L 6" With its longish tail, looks larger than the other *Empids*. Bill: rather long, two-colored. Wingtips shorter than Hammond's. Perches on low bushes, flying to the ground to catch insects. More gray but this is of no great help in identification in the field. Songs are short notes: repeated 'chu wip' and a sharp 'pwit' similar to the other *Empid* flycatchers.

Eastern Phoebe   xVa
Sayornis phoebe

L 7" Same size and habits as the Black Phoebe (p. 75), with a love for streamside habitats. When perched, wags its tail. Smudgey colored with a darker cap and faint wing bars. In the fall young birds have a yellowish cast on their belly.

Vermillion Flycatcher   xVa
Pyrocephalus rubinus

L 6" A guest from the hot south. Male, unmistakably brilliant red, with a dark mantle. Females always have some faint pink on their belly, are smaller and paler than the large Say's Phoebe (p. 75) and their breast is faintly streaked.

Eastern Kingbird   xVa
Tyrannus tyrannus

L 8½" Like the Western Kingbird (p. 76), perches on prominent open perches to watch for passing insects. A common bird throughout the eastern U.S. There is a single fall record in Napa County. Mainly gray and white with a black cap, and has a broad black and white-tipped tail, which is a good field mark. Has an orange-red crown stripe that is seldom visible.

Bohemian Waxwing   xV
Bombycilla garrulus

L 8¼" Irruptive in the winter, usually in flocks or together with Cedar Waxwings (p. 89), which they resemble but look larger and fat. The best field mark is the rufous undertail coverts which are white in the Cedar's. In flight, white marks are visible in wings, whereas the Cedar's wings are plain gray. Habits and voices are both very similar; the Bohemian calls are lower and harsher.

Brown Thrasher
Toxostoma rufum
xVa

L 11½" There is only one record of this eastern bird. It's unmistakable with its bright rufous colors, long rufous tail and stripes on breast. The California Thrasher (p. 88) has a longer, stronger, curved bill, is duller and more unicolored. The staring yellow eyes give the Brown a rather fierce expression.

Sage Thrasher
Oreoscoptes montanus
xVa ▷

L 8½" A western bird of sagebrush flats. Breeds in part of the California Sierra but is only a rare vagrant in Napa County with few records. Looks more like a thrush-colored mockingbird than a conventional thrasher. Unlike a thrush, has white tips to its dark tail. Is a ground feeder like all thrashers and thrushes.

American Tree Sparrow
Spizella arborea
xV

L 6¼" In the east they are called the 'winter chippy.' Breeds in the far north on shrubby tundra. Moves south in winter to open shrub country with some trees. Rarely reaching California. Similar to the smaller Chipping Sparrow (p. 94), a Napa breeder. Most distinctive are the bicolored bill, faint colors and dark spot on breast.

Chestnut-collared Longspur
Calcarius ornatus
xW

L 6" A dry prairie nester, which winters as far south as Mexico. Brightly colored in summer, but nondescript in winter when most likely to be seen in Napa. When watching a flock of Horned Larks (p. 98), look carefully to see if there's a Longspur amongst them. They are a bit smaller and have more white in their tail, clearly visible in flight.

♂ br Mar-Aug

♀

(see also p. 98)

Lapland Longspur
Calcarius lapponicus
xW ▷

L 6" Breeds in the open tundra of the entire northern hemisphere. In winter a regular in northern California but few venture farther south. The Dutch call them 'icebuntings.' Similar to the Chestnut-collared but a bit larger and much longer winged. Also mixes with Horned Lark flocks, often in open plowed fields. More likely to be observed in Napa than a Chestnut-collared.

♂ br Mar-Aug

♂ br Mar-Aug

♀

♂

Snow Bunting
Plectrophenax nivalis
xVa

L 6¾" Also a far northern breeder, but on more open, barren, rocky ground. In winter stays farther north but some come along the coast into California in late fall. Unmistakable in flight, with much white in the wings, except juv. Unlikely to see them in Napa in their br. dress; the nbr. dress is rather washed out. Also mixes with Horned Larks.

♂ nbr Aug-Mar

All these rare vagrants are not a regular part of the Napa County avifauna but it's always fascinating to find a new species not yet registered. Be very careful with your identifications.

Notes:

Cassin's Kingbird, sketch on p. 132

Checklist for the Birds of Napa County

This list contains all birds recorded in Napa County. They are listed in taxonomic order and each family is separated by a blue line.
The small box before each species allows you to keep a personal record of all birds sighted in the county. After the scientific name, the status of each species is denoted by a code, which is listed here for quick reference. The codes are explained in more detail on page 9.

c	common	x	extremely rare	P	Permanent resident	a	Autumn status
f	fairly common	i	irregular	S	Summer resident	s	Spring status
u	uncommon	l	limited	T	Transient	nbr.	non breeding
r	rare	ext.	extirpated	W	Winter resident	t	assumed breeder
				V	Vagrant	br.	breeding
							page

☐ Red-throated Loon	*Gavia stellata*	irW	20
☐ Pacific Loon	*pacifica*	xW	20
☐ Common Loon	*immer*	rW	20
☐ Pied-billed Grebe	*Podilymbus podiceps*	cW, uS	18
☐ Horned Grebe	*Podiceps auritus*	rW	18
☐ Red-necked Grebe	*grisegena*	ixW	18
☐ Eared Grebe	*nigricollis*	cW, lrS	18
☐ Western Grebe	*Aechmophorus occidentalis*	cW, luS	19
☐ Clark's Grebe	*clarkii*	lP	19
☐ Laysan Albatross	*Phoebastria immutabilis*	xV	114
☐ American White Pelican	*Pelecanus erythrorhynchos*	rW, fT,lS	21
☐ Brown Pelican	*occidentalis*	lxS	114
☐ Doubled-crested Cormorant	*Phalacrocorax auritus*	cW, luS	21
☐ American Bittern	*Botaurus lentiginosus*	lxPt	23
☐ Great Blue Heron	*Ardea herodias*	cP	23
☐ Great Egret	*alba*	cW, xS	23
☐ Snowy Egret	*Egretta thula*	cW, xS	23
☐ Cattle Egret	*Bubulcus ibis*	xW	114
☐ Green Heron	*Butorides virescens*	uW, fS	23
☐ Black-crowned Night-Heron	*Nycticorax nycticorax*	uP	23
☐ White-faced Ibis	*Plegadis chihi*	xW	114
☐ Turkey Vulture	*Cathartes aura*	cP	34
☐ California Condor	*Gymnogyps californianus*	extirpated	115
☐ Flamingo	*Phoenicopterus sp.*	escaped	112
☐ Greater White-fronted Goose	*Anser albifrons*	uW	25
☐ Snow Goose	*Chen caerulescens*	rW	25
☐ Ross's Goose	*rossii*	xV	25
☐ Canada Goose	*Branta canadensis*	cW, fS	24
☐ Cackling Goose	*hutchinsii*	irW	24
☐ Brant	*bernicla*	xTs	24
☐ Tundra Swan	*Cygnus columbianus*	irW	25
☐ Wood Duck	*Aix sponsa*	rP	26

☐ Mandarin Duck	*galericulata*	escaped	26
☐ Mallard	*Anas platyrhynchos*	cW, fS	26
☐ Gadwall	*strepera*	cW, luS	26
☐ American Wigeon	*americana*	cW	27
☐ Eurasian Wigeon	*penelope*	rW	27
☐ Blue-winged Teal	*discors*	xSnb	28
☐ Cinnamon Teal	*cyanoptera*	uW, lus	28
☐ Northern Shoveler	*clypeata*	cW, lxs	27
☐ Northern Pintail	*acuta*	cW, lrS	29
☐ Green-winged Teal	*crecca*	cW	28
☐ Canvasback	*Aythya valisineria*	cW, xSnb	30
☐ Redhead	*americana*	rW	30
☐ Ring-necked Duck	*collaris*	cW, xSnb	30
☐ Tufted Duck	*fuligula*	xW	30
☐ Greater Scaup	*marila*	fW, lxSnb	31
☐ Lesser Scaup	*affinis*	cW, lrS	31
☐ Surf Scoter	*Melanitta perspicillata*	lrW, xSnb	31
☐ White-winged Scoter	*fusca*	xTa	114
☐ Long-tailed Duck	*Clangula hyemalis*	ixTSnb	32
☐ Bufflehead	*Bucephala albeola*	cW, xSnb	32
☐ Common Goldeneye	*clangula*	fW, lxSnb	32
☐ Barrow's Goldeneye	*islandica*	xW	32
☐ Hooded Merganser	*Lophodytes cucullatus*	uW	33
☐ Common Merganser	*Mergus merganser*	uW, xS	33
☐ Red-breasted Merganser	*serrator*	xW	33
☐ Ruddy Duck	*Oxyura jamaicensis*	cW, xS	32
☐ Osprey	*Pandion haliaetus*	rP	34
☐ White-tailed Kite	*Elanus leucurus*	uP	36
☐ Bald Eagle	*Haliaetus leucocephalus*	rW, xS	35
☐ Northern Harrier	*Circus cyaneus*	uW, lrs	36
☐ Sharp-shinned Hawk	*Accipiter striatus*	uW, xS	37
☐ Cooper's Hawk	*cooperii*	uW, rS	37
☐ Northern Goshawk	*gentilis*	ixV	37
☐ Red-shouldered Hawk	*Buteo lineatus*	fP	38-40
☐ Swainson's Hawk	*swainsoni*	xS	38-40
☐ Red-tailed Hawk	*jamaicensis*	cW, fS	39-40
☐ Ferruginous Hawk	*regalis*	rW	39-41
☐ Rough-legged Hawk	*agopus*	rW	40
☐ Golden Eagle	*Aquila chrysaetos*	uW, rS	35
☐ American Kestrel	*Falco sparverius*	cW, fS	44
☐ Merlin	*columbarius*	rW	44
☐ Peregrine Falcon	*peregrinus*	xW, lrP	45

☐ Prairie Falcon	*mexicanus*	lrP	45
☐ Mountain Quail	*Oreortyx pictus*	fP	46
☐ California Quail	*Callipepla californica*	cP	46
☐ Ring-necked Pheasant	*Phasianus colchicus*	uP, introduced	46
☐ Wild Turkey	*Meleagris gallopavo*	fP, introduced	47
☐ Black Rail	*Laterallus jamaicensis*	lrP	49
☐ Clapper Rail	*Rallus longirostris*	lrP	49
☐ Virginia Rail	*limicola*	luP	49
☐ Sora	*Porzana carolina*	elrP	48
☐ Common Moorhen	*Gallinula chloropus*	lrP	48
☐ American Coot	*Fulica americana*	cW, rS	48
☐ Sandhill Crane	*Grus canadensis*	xTa	115
☐ Black-bellied Plover	*Pluvialis squatarola*	fW	50
☐ American Golden Plover	*dominica*	lxT	50
☐ Pacific Golden Plover	*fulva*	lxT	50
☐ Snowy Plover	*Charadrius alexandrinus*	lrS	50
☐ Semipalmated Plover	*semipalmatus*	luW	50
☐ Killdeer	*vociferus*	cW, fS	51
☐ Black-necked Stilt	*Himantopus mexicanus*	luW, lrS	51
☐ American Avocet	*Recurvirostra americana*	lfW, lrS	51
☐ Greater Yellowlegs	*Tringa melanoleuca*	uW, Snb	52
☐ Lesser Yellowlegs	*flavipes*	xW, rTa	52
☐ Solitary Sandpiper	*solitaria*	xVs	115
☐ Willet	*Catoptrophorus semipalmatus*	fW	52
☐ Spotted Sandpiper	*Actitis macularia*	rP	52
☐ Whimbrel	*Numenius phaeopus*	rTS	53
☐ Long-billed Curlew	*americanus*	uW, xSnb	53
☐ Marbled Godwit	*Limosa fedoa*	fW, xSnb	52
☐ Ruddy Turnstone	*Arenaria interpres*	xTa	53
☐ Red Knot	*Calidris canutus*	xW, xTSnb	54
☐ Sanderling	*alba*	xW	54
☐ Semipalmated Sandpiper	*pusilla*	xTa	115
☐ Western Sandpiper	*mauri*	fW, cTS, fTa	54
☐ Least Sandpiper	*minutilla*	fW, cTS, fTa	54
☐ Baird's Sandpiper	*bairdii*	lxTa	54
☐ Pectoral Sandpiper	*melanotos*	lrTa	55
☐ Dunlin	*alpina*	fW, cTS, rTa	55
☐ Ruff	*Philomachus pugnax*	xTa	115
☐ Short-billed Dowitcher	*Limnodromus griseus*	rTa	53
☐ Long-billed Dowitcher	*scolopaceus*	fW,cT	53
☐ Wilson's Snipe	*Gallinago delicata*	uW	53
☐ Wilson's Phalarope	*Phalaropus tricolor*	xW, exS, lrTa	55

☐ Red-necked Phalarope	*obatus*	rTs	55
☐ Red Phalarope	*fulicarius*	xTa	55
☐ Parasitic Jaeger	*Stercorarius parasiticus*	xW	115
☐ Franklin's Gull	*Larus pipixcan*	xV	115
☐ Little Gull	*minutus*	xV	115
☐ Bonaparte's Gull	*philadelphia*	uW, xSnb	60
☐ Mew Gull	*canus*	fW	58-60
☐ Ring-billed Gull	*delawarensis*	cW, xSnb	58
☐ California Gull	*californicus*	cW, rSnb	58
☐ Herring Gull	*argentatus*	cW, rSnb	58
☐ Thayer's Gull	*thayeri*	rW	59
☐ Western Gull	*occidentalis*	uW, rSnb	59
☐ Glaucous-winged Gull	*glaucescens*	cW	59
☐ Glaucous Gull	*hyperboreus*	xW	59
☐ Black-legged Kittiwake	*Rissa tridactyla*	xW	60
☐ Caspian Tern	*Sterna caspia*	fSnb	61
☐ Elegant Tern	*elegans*	xTa	115
☐ Common Tern	*hirundo*	xTa	115
☐ Forster's Tern	*forsteri*	lfS	61
☐ Least Tern	*antillarum*	xTa	61
☐ Black Tern	*Chlidonias niger*	xT	61
☐ Rock Dove	*Columba livia*	cP	62
☐ Band-tailed Pigeon	*fasciata*	iuP	62
☐ Mourning Dove	*Zenaida macroura*	cP	62
☐ Yellow-billed Cuckoo	*Coccyzus americanus*	extirpated	116
☐ Greater Roadrunner	*Geococcyx californicus*	rP	63
☐ Barn Owl	*Tyto alba*	cP	64
☐ Flammulated Owl	*Otus flammeolus*	xTa	66
☐ Western Screech Owl	*kennicottii*	cP	66
☐ Great Horned Owl	*Bubo virginianus*	cP	65
☐ Northern Pygmy-Owl	*Glaucidium gnoma*	uP	66
☐ Burrowing Owl	*Athene cunicularia*	rW, extirpated	67
☐ Spotted Owl	*Strix occidentalis*	uP	65
☐ Barred Owl	*varia*	uP, ?S	65
☐ Long-eared Owl	*Asio otus*	rW, lxS	64
☐ Short-eared Owl	*flammeus*	xPub	64
☐ Northern Saw-whet Owl	*Aegolius acadicus*	rP	66
☐ Lesser Nighthawk	*Chordeiles acutipennis*	xT	67
☐ Common Nighthawk	*minor*	xTs	67
☐ Common Poorwill	*Phalaenoptilus nuttallii*	xW, uS	67
☐ Black Swift	*Cypseloides niger*	ixT	68
☐ Vaux's Swift	*Chaetura vauxi*	uTs, rTa	68

☐ Clark's Nutcracker	*Nucifraga columbiana*	xTa	111
☐ Yellow-billed Magpie	*Pica nuttalli*	rP	78
☐ Black-billed Magpie	*hudsonia*	X?	78
☐ American Crow	*Corvus brachyrhynchos*	cP	78
☐ Common Raven	*corax*	fP	78
☐ Horned Lark	*Eremophila alpestris*	uP	98
☐ Purple Martin	*Progne subis*	lrS	80
☐ Tree Swallow	*Tachycineta bicolor*	irW, cS	80
☐ Violet-Green Swallow	*thalassina*	xW, cS	80
☐ North. Rough-winged Swallow	*Stelgidopteryx serripennis*	fS	81
☐ Bank Swallow	*Riparia riparia*	eS, xT	81
☐ Cliff Swallow	*Petrochelidon pyrrhonota*	cS	81
☐ Barn Swallow	*Hirundo rustica*	cS	81
☐ Mountain Chickadee	*Poecile gambeli*	xTa	82
☐ Chestnut-backed Chickadee	*fusescens*	fP	82
☐ Oak Titmouse	*Baeolophus inornatus*	cP	82
☐ Bushtit	*Psaltriparus minimus*	cP	82
☐ Red-breasted Nuthatch	*Sitta canadensis*	iuW, rS	83
☐ White-breasted Nuthatch	*arolinensis*	cP	83
☐ Pygmy Nuthatch	*pygmaea*	fW, uS	83
☐ Brown Creeper	*Certhia americana*	fP	84
☐ Rock Wren	*Salipinctes obsoletus*	uP	85
☐ Canyon Wren	*Catherpes mexicanus*	uP	85
☐ Bewick's Wren	*Thryomanes bewickii*	cP	85
☐ House Wren	*Troglodytes aedon*	rW, cS	84
☐ Winter Wren	*troglodytes*	uP	84
☐ Marsh Wren	*Cistothorus palustris*	fP	84
☐ American Dipper	*Cinclus mexicanus*	rW, LxS	89
☐ Golden-crowned Kinglet	*Regulus satrapa*	uW	90
☐ Ruby-crowned Kinglet	*calendula*	cW	90
☐ Blue-gray Gnatcatcher	*Polioptila caerulea*	fS	90
☐ Western Bluebird	*Sialia mexicana*	fS	86
☐ Mountain Bluebird	*currucoides*	xW	111
☐ Townsend's Solitaire	*Myadestes townsendi*	luW	111
☐ Swainson's Thrush	*Catharus ustulatus*	uS	86
☐ Hermit Thrush	*guttatus*	cW, uS	86
☐ American Robin	*Turdus migratoris*	cW, fS	87
☐ Varied Thrush	*Ixoreus naevius*	uW	87
☐ Wrentit	*Chamaea fasciata*	fP	85
☐ Northern Mockingbird	*Mimus polyglottos*	cP	88
☐ Sage Thrasher	*Oreoscoptes montanus*	xVa	117
☐ Brown Thrasher	*Toxostoma rufum*	xVa	117

☐ Golden-crowned Sparrow	*atricapilla*	cWT	97
☐ Dark-eyed Junco	*Junco hyemalis*	cW, fS	96
☐ Lapland Longspur	*Calcarius lapponicus*	xW	98, 117
☐ Chestnut-collared Longspur	*ornatus*	xW	98, 117
☐ Snow Bunting	*Plectrophenax nivalis*	xVa	117
☐ Rose-breasted Grosbeak	*Pheucticus ludovicianus*	xT	99
☐ Black-headed Grosbeak	*melanocephalus*	fS	99
☐ Blue Grosbeak	*Guiraca caerulea*	xTS	99
☐ Lazuli Bunting	*Passerina amoena*	rS	99
☐ Indigo Bunting	*cyanea*	xTS	99
☐ Bobolink	*Dolichonyx oryzivorus*	xTa	101
☐ Red-winged Blackbird	*Agelaius phoeniceus*	cP	100
☐ Bicolored Blackbird	*mailliadorum*	cP	100
☐ Tricolored Blackbird	*tricolor*	rW, lfS	100
☐ Yellow-headed Blackbird	*Xanthocephalus xanthocephalus*	LxS	101
☐ Western Meadowlark	*Sturnella neglecta*	cP	101
☐ Brewer's Blackbird	*Euphagus cyanocephalus*	cP	102
☐ Great-tailed Grackle	*Quiscalus mexicanus*	xNb	102
☐ Brown-headed Cowbird	*Molothrus ater*	rW, uS	103
☐ Hooded Oriole	*Icterus cucullatus*	rS	104
☐ Bullock's Oriole	*bullockii*	cS	104
☐ Orchard Oriole	*spurius*	xW	104
☐ Evening Grosbeak	*Coccothraustes verpertinus*	irW, ixTS	106
☐ House Finch	*Carpodacus mexicanus*	cP	106
☐ Purple Finch	*purpureus*	uP	106
☐ Cassin's Finch	*cassinii*	xTa	111
☐ Red Crossbill	*Loxia curvirostra*	irW, ixSnb	106
☐ Pine Siskin	*Carduelis pinus*	fW, xST	107
☐ American Goldfinch	*tristis*	P	107
☐ Lesser Goldfinch	*psaltria*	cP	107
☐ Lawrence's Goldfinch	*lawrencei*	xW, LS	107
☐ House Sparrow	*Passer domesticus*	cP	98

There is always the possibility you may find a bird not listed in this book. Please forward a sighting not listed to the Napa-Solano Audubon Society, P.O. Box 5027, Vallejo, CA 94591. Include a complete description of your observation, the date and precise locality, and how you may be contacted.

Index

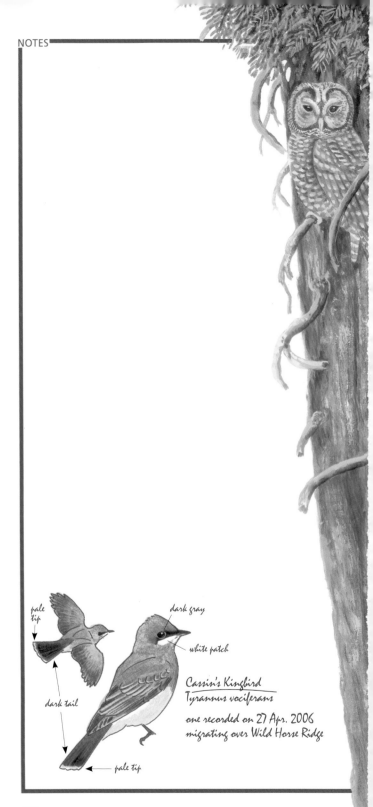

pale tip

dark gray

white patch

dark tail

Cassin's Kingbird
Tyrannus vociferans

one recorded on 27 Apr. 2006
migrating over Wild Horse Ridge

pale tip